Osprey Modelling • 2

Modelling the Challenger 1 and 2 MBT and Variants

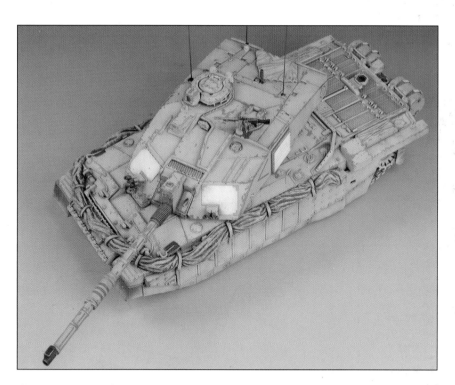

Graeme Davidson & Pat Johnston

Consultant editor Robert Oehler • *Series editors* Marcus Cowper and Nikolai Bogdanovic

First published in 2006 by Osprey Publishing
Midland House, West Way, Botley, Oxford OX2 0PH, UK
443 Park Avenue South, New York, NY 10016, USA
E-mail: info@ospreypublishing.com

ISBN 1 84176 927 4

Page layout by Servis Filmsetting Ltd, Manchester, UK
Index by Alison Worthington
Typeset in Monotype Gill Sans and ITC Sans Serif
Originated by Solidity Graphics, Prague, Czech Republic
Printed and bound in China through Bookbuilders

06 07 08 09 10   10 9 8 7 6 5 4 3 2 1

A CIP catalogue record for this book is available from the British Library.

FOR A CATALOGUE OF ALL BOOKS PUBLISHED BY OSPREY MILITARY
AND AVIATION PLEASE CONTACT:

NORTH AMERICA
Osprey Direct, C/O Random House Distribution Center, 400 Hahn Road, Westminster,
MD 21157, USA
E-mail: info@ospreydirectusa.com

ALL OTHER REGIONS
Osprey Direct UK, P.O. Box 140, Wellingborough, Northants, NN8 2FA, UK
E-mail: info@ospreydirect.co.uk

Photographic credits

Unless otherwise indicated, the author took all the photographs
in this work.

Acknowledgements

Thanks to Derek Hansen of Accurate Armour, Gilles Pfeiffer of
Blast Models, Lawrence Goh of Echelon Fine Details, and
Giuseppe Puppato of Friulmodellismo for their generosity and
support.

Thanks to Sam Dwyer, Bob Griffon, Dan Hay, Willy Nailor,
Luigi Pittino, Gordon Cobban, Jan Willem DeBoer, Simon
Dunstan and all the lads at *Die Schlangengrube* for their help
with research, technical advice, spare parts and words of
encouragement.

Special thanks to Pat Johnston, who, armed with an airbrush,
a pack of smokes and a half tank of gas, rescued this book at the
11th hour. Pat's excellent airbrush and weathering talent appear
on the two 1/72-scale kits, the KFOR Challenger 1 Mk 3 and
the fantastic chipping work on the UNPROFOR CrARRV.
Cheers, bud!

Contents

Introduction   4

Challenger 1 Mk 3, Kings Royal Hussars,   5
Op Agricola c.1999
Background • Construction • Painting and weathering

Challenger 2, Royal Scots Dragoon Guards,   17
Op Telic c.2003
Background • Construction • Painting and weathering

Challenger 1 Mk 3, 4th Armoured Brigade,   24
Op Granby c.1991
Background • Construction • Painting and weathering

Desert Challenger 2, 1st Tank Regiment,   32
Royal Army of Oman, Ex 'Saif Sareea II' c.2001
Background • Construction • Painting and weathering

Challenger Armoured Repair & Recovery Vehicle,   45
32 Regt RE, Op Grapple, United Nations Protection Force,
Bosnia-Herzegovina c.1995
Background • Construction • Painting and weathering

Challenger 2, Royal Dragoon Guards, Op Telic c.2005   53
Background • Construction • Painting and weathering

Falcon 2 AB9C5, 7th Tank Battalion,   64
99th Armoured Brigade, Jordanian Army
Background • Construction • Painting and weathering

Gallery   76

Further reading   78
Armour modelling websites • Reference websites

Kits and accessories   79
Injection-moulded Challenger kits • Detail sets

Index   80

Introduction

Introduced to the British Army in 1983, Challenger Main Battle Tanks have served operationally in the Balkans and both Gulf Wars, where their firepower, protection and shock action were instrumental to the success of British forces.

In addition to the familiar gun tanks, the Challenger family encompasses the Rhino Armoured Repair & Recovery Vehicle (ARRV), the highly modified Desert Challenger 2s operated by the Royal Army of Oman, and the radical Falcon 2 being developed by the Jordanian Army.

As the tank is well represented by major kit manufacturers in both 1/72 and 1/35 scales, this book covers a wide range of the Challenger family from Tamiya, Revell, Trumpeter and Accurate Armour, along with a helping of scratch-built and commercially available detail and marking sets.

I have tried to include as many different versions of the Challenger as possible in this book. As a result, there are seven chapters describing the construction and painting of these various tanks. I have attempted to prescribe a 'difficulty rating' to each chapter, but that is very much a subjective assessment and, as the saying goes, your mileage may vary. More advanced builders may question why I did not add certain details or fix a particular error in a kit. The reason is that in some of the chapters, I have deliberately kept the builds to what I consider an 'intermediate level' and these are marked with either one or two stars. However, even the four-star chapters should be within the skill set of an intermediate modeller; if you can scratch build a square box then you are 90 per cent of the way there already! Unfortunately, the five-star build for this book never came to be – I had wanted to include a Trojan AEV but real life got in the way. In its place, I have substituted an extra two chapters on what I think are interesting variants – the Falcon 2 used by Jordan and the newly up-armoured Challenger 2 with modifications to counter the close-combat threats in Iraq.

In order to allow enough space to adequately describe all seven chapters and still keep this book to 80 pages, I have had to find space in other areas. For that reason, there are no lists describing tools, museums and nomenclature. If I've used a specific tool it is mentioned in the relevant chapter. In order to save room within the model chapters, I have tried to avoid repeating the explanation of a technique used. Most times, a specific technique is depicted once, and if it is used again, I will refer you to the chapter in which it is described.

Challenger 1 Mk 3, Kings Royal Hussars, Op Agricola c.1999

Construction and photography by Graeme Davidson
Finishing by Pat Johnston

Degree of Difficulty:	★★★☆☆
Kits used:	*Tamiya Challenger 1 Mk 3 (35154), Accurate Armour Challenger Combat Dozer (A032).*
Additional detailing sets used:	*Eduard photo-etch for Challenger 1 (35332), Scale Scenics mesh, Aber photo-etch Chains, Numbers, cheese cloth, .22g copper wire, .24g floral wire, various Evergreen styrene and Tichy bolt sets.*
Markings:	*Echelon Fine Details' Challenger 1 Decals (T35002), kit decals.*
Paints:	*Tamiya XF-67 NATO Green, XF-62 Olive Drab, XF-69 NATO Black, XF-2 White, XF-3 Yellow, XF-7 Red and XF-57 Buff; Humbrol Matt 49, 75 and 33; Testors' Chrome Silver; Winsor & Newton Raw Umber, Yellow Ochre, Lamp Black and White; Rembrandt Raw Umber pastel chalk.*
References:	*Osprey New Vanguard 23:* Challenger MBT 1982–97, Jane's Armour and Artillery 2003, *Concord 7505* Challenger 1 & 2.

Background

The Challenger 1 began its service in the British Army following the failure to deliver the Shir 2 that was originally designed for Iran prior to the overthrow of the Shah. Following that event, Royal Ordnance was tasked to build 243 Challenger 1s (FV 4030/3) for the British Army in spring of 1983, with the Royal Tank Regiment (RTR) receiving the first tanks later the following year. The Challenger has only gone through a few upgrades over its service life, with a Mk 3 Challenger being the final version that has been fitted with a Thermal Observation and Gunnery Sight (TOGS) (Mk 2) and a quick release for the rear-mounted fuel drums. In 1990, the Pearson Combat Dozer Blade (UDK1) was accepted for service and all Challengers were capable of mounting it. The dozer was used to dig hull-down fighting positions, clear obstacles and fill in anti-tank ditches. This chapter depicts a Challenger dozer tank of the KRH Regiment deployed to Kosovo as part of the NATO Operation Joint Guardian contingent in 1999. This would be the last operational deployment for the Challenger 1, as the following year the British Army would take delivery of the new Challenger 2.

Construction

First introduced as a Challenger 1 Mk 2 kit (35134), Tamiya later released the kit following the 1991 Gulf War and included additional parts to build the up-armoured version with external long-range fuel tanks. Out of the box, it builds into a decent kit; however, there are three main areas that can be improved upon with a bit of scratch-building: the turret bin, the fuel-drum mounts and

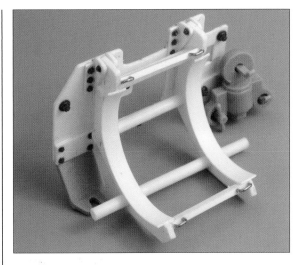

ABOVE Holes were drilled into each cross bar for the brass wire tie-down brackets.

LEFT The kit external fuel-drum brackets were replaced by scratch-built items.

Side appliqué armour was spaced away from the hull. If only Tamiya's Challenger 2 had been released when I worked on this, I could have saved a lot of effort!

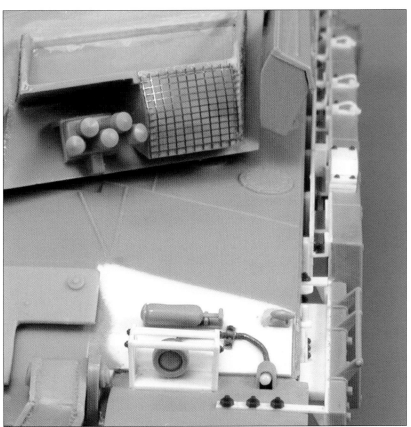

the side armour. While this conversion is primarily focused on these areas, I will also mention some of the extra detailing added to other parts of the kit.

The first step was to rebuild the fuel-drum mounts, which consist of a pair of curved brackets cut from .020in. plastic strip mounted to a plate cut from .010in. plastic sheet. Instead of trying to cut the curve with an X-Acto, I outlined the shape on the plastic using a pencil and then removed the excess with a drum sander mounted in a Dremel tool. This method can quickly melt the plastic, so I hooked up a sewing machine pedal to my Dremel. This permits the machine to turn slower and not build sufficient heat to melt the styrene. My Dremel tool is a

Tow cable brackets were rebuilt and relocated.

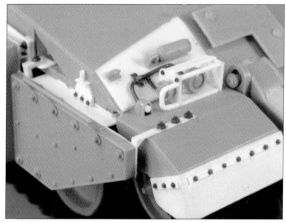

The front hull was levelled off with .030in. sheet and the light guards and mud flaps were rebuilt. An indicator light was made from rounded styrene rod.

single-speed type; I have read that you should not attempt to hook up a speed controller to a Dremel with the five-speed selection as it can damage the motor.

Once I had made four matching brackets (I think I had to make about ten before I got four the same size!), I drilled three holes in each side into which I inserted three rods. On the real Challengers, these rods are actually tubes, so once they were in place, I drilled out the end of each rod to a depth of a few millimetres, giving the impression of a hollow tube.

In between each end of the curved bracket, a rectangular strip was inserted and four holes drilled into each edge. The holes provide a secure mount to glue some 26g brass wire, bent into a C-shape using a pair of needle-nose pliers. These wires are where the straps to hold the fuel drum are attached.

With each pair of brackets done, I could fix them to the mounting plate and add various sizes of Tichy bolts. The only tricky part on the mounting plate was the inside cuts. These were cut somewhat undersized to allow for expansion when I tidied up the edges using a square metal file. Also added to the base plate were some of the tank recovery parts shaved from the Tamiya kit. I also shaved the fuel strap ratchet buckles from the kit drums. These were set aside for attaching to some lead foil straps later on. Some of the KFOR Challengers I've seen did not carry the extra fuel tanks, so I decided to leave them empty with just the straps in place.

The side armour was the next part of the hull to be detailed. When I started this kit, the Tamiya Challenger 2 had not yet been released – what a time saver it would have been as the side armour on the Challenger 2 is done really well; unfortunately the Challenger 1 is quite simplified and does not have the correctly spaced mount and hangers. The first step was to back the Tamiya panels with some sheet styrene. This gave a good gluing surface for the rest of the mounts. The hull received some .020in. strip, which, spaced at intervals, supported a long sheet of plastic card running the length of the hull. On to the face of this were attached several L-shaped strips cut into segments. The rear bazooka plates were made with .020in. stock and detailed with brass wire tie-down loops. What took one paragraph to describe took several hours of research, a couple days of building and is still not 100 per cent accurate! I'm not certain, but I think the Challenger 2 armour from the Tamiya kit might be the best fix for this kit. Once in place, I scratch-built the tow cable lead housings and cable clamps that were attached to the side armour. These clamps were detailed with short segments of rod and discs from the punch and die set. That was the two hardest parts of the hull done, and now I could work on some smaller details.

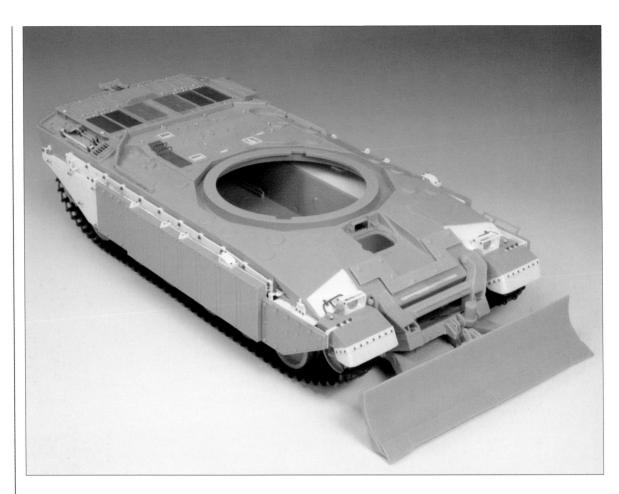

Accurate Armour Pearson Dozer blade is test-fitted, while the rear hull deck gets the grab handles replaced and some Eduard photo-etch screens.

Turret tie-downs were replaced with brass wire and corner reinforcements were made with butt-joined strips of styrene.

Track tools were replaced and relocated to the turret roof, and the vehicle ID numbers were cut from an Aber photo-etch set.

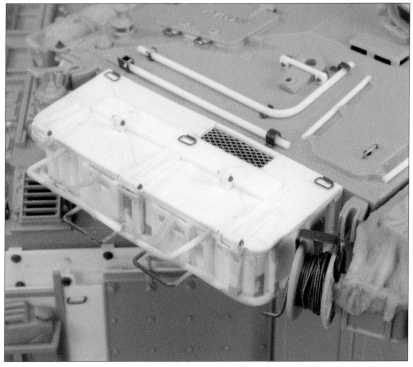

The rear turret bin was rebuilt with the correct square shape and detailed with brass mesh, copper wire and Tamiya tape.

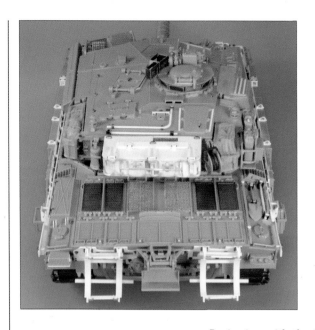

ABOVE Deck screens are a mix of Tamiya photo-etch and Scenics brass mesh.

LEFT Side bins had covers made from rolled Apoxie Sculpt draped over some scrap boxes and gas cans.

Beginning with the front hull, I levelled off the glacis plate by adding some bevel-cut .030in. plastic squares. I'm not sure why Tamiya moulded the centre of the glacis plate proud of the flanks, but it is incorrect for this version. The headlight mounts were also rebuilt using .010in. sheet, strip and .020in. rod for the tubular brackets. The signal light was also formed from .020in. rod and given a light sanding round the edges to make it look more like a lens. Some lead solder was inserted into each driving and signal light and, on the left side, the horn was also wired. The front mud flaps were made with .010in. sheet; these were tacked in place using cyanoacrylate (CA) glue at one corner. Once dry, the top edge of the mud flap was bent around the lower lip of the hull fender part. This was done using CA glue and a clamp to fix the part as it was curved round the fender. The top edge of the flap was detailed with a strip of bolts on the front and each side.

The top rear of the hull was next up, with some Eduard screens for the deck and some Scale Scenics brass mesh for the centre grilles. The deck sitting under the rear turret overhang also got some grab handle pockets drilled out and some panel lines were rescribed for the correct hatch outline. Each of the hinge ends for the deck grilles received a small punch and die bolt head, as did the hinged ends on the fuel filler caps. Some brackets were pulled from an Eduard set and the pioneer tools attached. I contemplated replacing the moulded-on engine deck handles with brass wire, but I decided that this was an effort that might cause more harm than good, in that it would be very easy to damage the surrounding grille louvres. So I moved on to the dozer blade. The AA dozer blade was assembled per instructions with no difficulty, except I sanded and filled a seam that I shouldn't have! The top edge of the blade and the trapezoid-shaped plate is supposed to have a slight gap at the join line. Just a note that in these in-progress photos, the glacis armour plate is not permanently attached.

Work on the turret began with replacing the large rear storage bin. There's only two tricky bits to this part – getting the curved corners at the rear, and remembering that the lid has a gentle slope to the rear. I managed to build a complete bin before realizing this! For the rounded edges I just doubled up a layer of .040in. sheet and used CA to hold it. That way, I could just sand a curved radius without fear of going right through the plastic. The top and bottom edge of the bin was trimmed with styrene rod and the sides detailed with some strips. The fuel-can bracket at the rear of the bin was made with .020in. rod; again I drilled a small hole in the C bracket and the base for the 45-degree supporting

Weld beads made from stretched and textured sprue were shaped around the base of the front turret lifting lugs. The front armour plate is not attached yet – see the painted photos for the correct location.

LEFT AND BELOW LEFT The completed model prior to painting.

bar. Copper wire was used for the base of the fuel can support. The straps that secure the top of the fuel cans were made from Tamiya tape cut into thin strips and brushed with CA glue to add rigidity. The end of the tape straps was looped around a small bracket made from stretched sprue. The last detail was cutting out a small rectangle in the forward edge of the lid, under which I added some brass mesh. I assume this is for air circulation for whatever is stashed away in the bin.

Some of the maintenance tools were relocated to the turret roof; these were made with styrene rod for the simple reason that I couldn't be bothered scraping the seams off the kit parts! Small brackets for these tools come with the Eduard set, and were enhanced by short lengths of wire.

The rear turret hatch was detailed with some Aber brass numbers to create a purely fictional Fighting Vehicle (FV) number for the tank. The moulded-on handles were chiselled off and replaced with thin copper wire. Other small tie-down handles throughout the turret (about two dozen roughly) were replaced with 26g brass wire. The side stowage bins were filled with some scrap plastic and then covered with a tarp made from a thin sheet of rolled Apoxie Sculpt.

The commander's cupola had the Eduard ammo can bracket added for the GPMG. This is designed to hold three 7.62mm ammo cans and is one of the nicer parts in the Eduard kit. The glass in the commander's optics was made with red, violet and gold foils designed to simulate the varying reflective properties of the laser filter coating.

The turret area around the TOGS was reinforced with welded brackets. On the model, these serrated brackets were done first by attaching thin strips and then adding the 'teeth' at even intervals along each edge.

Around the base of each of the front turret lifting lugs, a stretched sprue bead was glued and textured with a soldering iron on low heat. This makes a welded-on effect, and also has the added advantage of filling the gaps at the base of the part. The cam net bin had etch from the Eduard set added, and a cam net made from cheesecloth was stuffed inside. For the gun barrel, I scraped undercuts on each strap and fold on the thermal shroud with the backside of a No. 11 blade. This helped enhance the strap detail in the painting process later on.

Painting and weathering

The KFOR Challengers were finished in the standard UK pattern of broad bands of black over a green base. After masking off the optics, painting began using Tamiya NATO Green mixed with equal parts of Olive Drab. This makes a close match to British green, but as this colour tends to vary a fair bit in real life, you don't need to get too hung up on mixing an exact match. The black bands were done with Tamiya NATO Black sprayed through a Badger 200 single-action brush with a fine tip. The Tamiya paint can spray quite well through this brush so long as it is thinned with around 30–40 per cent thinner. I have found Tamiya's own brand of thinner works best with these paints.

I realized after painting the camouflage that I probably should have painted the orange air ID panel first! To paint the panel, I removed the turret from the kit and masked off everywhere that I did not want orange paint to go. I first sprayed a coat of Tamiya Flat White on to provide a good base for the orange. I believe the white basecoat is the same technique used on the real vehicles. The orange was mixed by adding a few drops of Tamiya Red to Tamiya Yellow – not that there is anything wrong with Tamiya Orange, other than I didn't have any in my paint rack. This mix was sprayed on in a few coats at low pressure to avoid any paint creeping under the masking tape. Photographing the orange paint is a bit difficult as it seems to over-saturate the meter on my digital camera.

Next up I applied the decals from the Echelon set. These are among the finest decals I have ever used. They sit perfectly flat, are printed in great register and have among the best instruction sheets I have seen. Moreover, you get lots of spare call-signs to model a specific vehicle, which in this case of depicting a dozer-equipped tank was a necessity. I was able to make the correct squadron

The base camouflage colours and decals have been applied. The weathering on the dozer blade was done using the same method as the wear on the CrARRV.

The orange panel on the bin is a common feature on S/KFOR vehicles to assist with air–ground identification.

The Echelon Fine Details' markings are printed beautifully and went on with ease.

Fuel-drum straps were fashioned from Tamiya tape and attached to the ratcheting buckles shaved from the kit part.

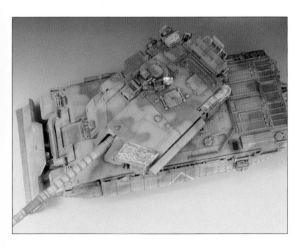

The camouflage net bin was covered with some tissue paper dipped in white glue, washed with oils and drybrushed with Humbrol enamels.

The engine deck was given a light drybrushing of Humbrol Matt 75 and white to pick out the grille and grab handle details.

A stubby bristled paintbrush was flicked near the tracks to show splashes of mud.

Deck tan paint, heavily thinned, was sprayed along the lower half of the hull.

Violet, red and gold foil was used to represent the shifting colours of the anti-laser coating on the optics.

ABOVE AND BELOW LEFT Accurate Armour water bottles moulded in clear resin and a Maple Leaf Models' map of Bosnia occupy the GMPG ammo bins.

The straps on the 120mm gun were undercut slightly with the back side of a No. 11 blade. The dozer blade was given a wipe of pencil lead to simulate exposed metal.

indicator and the A Squadron, second-in-command 'Zero Charlie' call sign with the sheet markings.

The dozer blade received a slightly different paint treatment. First, I painted it a dark steel grey and applied some liquid masking fluid (the technique is described later in the book), which was then overpainted with green. I mixed a slightly different shade of green as it appeared that some dozer blades were painted at different times and weathered at a different rate than the tank they were attached to. After painting, the latex mask was rubbed off using a pencil eraser. It gives a nice chipped effect when done. The tracks were given a quick coat of flat earth to provide a base colour on which to weather. Once all the decals were on, I sealed them with some Humbrol flat coat (Matt 49) and set the kit aside to dry for a few days before starting to weather.

I began the weathering process by given the model several washes of Winsor & Newton oils using Raw Umber, Lamp Black, Yellow Ochre and White. Additionally, these colours were mixed to form a dusty grey-brown that was applied as a pin wash to the details below engine-deck level. Following this, I drybrushed the green areas with a mix of Humbrol 75 and white, and the black areas with a grey mix of lamp black and white. The paint chips were made using a grey pencil crayon and the shadowing was made with dark brown pastel dust applied with a 0 brush. The spills around the fuel caps were applied with heavily diluted lamp black plus Humbrol Gloss Clear to impart a slightly wet look. The commander's GPMG was first painted flat black and then the metal areas were given a light drybrushing of chrome silver and a raw umber oil paint wash.

BELOW AND OVERLEAF
Overall view. Paint chips were added to the surface using a green pencil crayon while shadows were enhanced with dark brown pigment dust applied dry with a fine brush.

Challenger 2, Royal Scots Dragoon Guards, Op Telic c.2003

Construction and photography by Graeme Davidson	
Finishing by Pat Johnston	
Degree of Difficulty:	★☆☆☆☆
Kit used:	*DML Challenger 2 Iraq 2003 (7228).*
Additional detailing sets used:	*Extratech photo-etch set for Challenger 2 (72079), Apoxie Sculpt.*
Markings:	*Kit supplied.*
Paints:	*Tamiya Acrylics XF-60 Dark Yellow, XF-67 NATO Green, XF-65 Field Grey, XF-2 Flat White, XF-3 Flat Yellow, XF-7 Flat Red, XF-69 NATO Black, XF-55 Deck Tan and XF-57 Buff; Humbrol 67 and 75; Mig Pigments 023 Smoke and 027 Light Dust, and Rembrandt Raw Umber pastel chalk.*
References:	*Jane's Armour and Artillery 2003, Concord: 7505 Challenger 1 & 2, 7805 Journal of Assault & Heliborne Warfare, 5525 Special Ops.*

Background

Vickers Defence Systems began work on the Challenger 2 back in 1986 as a replacement for the Challenger 1. Development continued through the late 1980s and an order for 127 gun tanks was placed in 1991 with an additional 259 being ordered in 1994. In January 2003 the British Army deployed to Iraq under the codename Operation Telic. The 7th Armoured Brigade with their Challenger 2s from the Scots DG and 2 RTR, with QRL reinforcing, saw tank action while securing Basra in March of that year. Prior to the deployment, several modifications were installed on some 116 Challenger 2s. These included an upgraded armour package, extended side skirts, exhaust covers and an improved air-filtration system. The DML kit depicts a gun tank of 1st Troop, C Squadron, Scots DG, which is the only marking option included with the kit. I've depicted this model after the fighting for Basra some time in April 2003.

Construction

The DML kit arrived in 2004, around the same time as their die-cast versions of this tank. The moulding is good for 1/72 scale, but not as crisp as a Revell production. However, it is the only styrene kit of the Cr 2 in this scale so I thought it would be interesting to build and compare it to the Revell Cr 1 also in 1/72 scale. This kit was my first return to 1/72 scale after building a Matchbox Firefly back in 1981, it was fun to try this scale even though it signalled that I definitely need reading glasses!

There is not much to write about the construction; the parts fit very well throughout, with the only gripe being the vinyl tracks that seem a bit too tight. This tightness causes the track pads to bow in and form a convex shape between the teeth of the drive sprocket. However, the rear mud flaps cover this area, so it's a moot point if you are building an Op Telic Challenger.

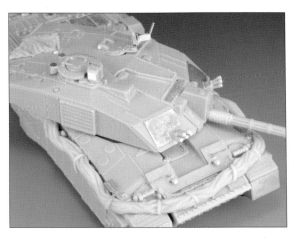

A thin roll of Apoxie Sculpt was used for the tarp and an air ID panel. Folds were made using dental picks and the tie-down straps were cut using a straight razor on putty that had been allowed to cure for about 10 minutes.

Fine copper speaker wire formed the power cable for the headlights.

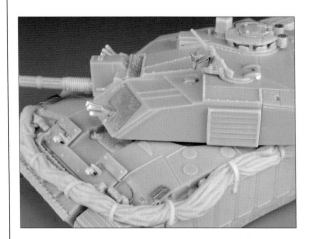

ABOVE, ABOVE RIGHT AND RIGHT The Extratech photo-etch kit comes with a belt of etched 7.62mm cartridges and very fine handles for the engine deck. Also included were the latch handles for the fuel-drum straps; however, I managed to lose one of them and had to swap ones shaved from the Revell Cr 1 kit. The rear edges of the TECs and sand skirts were shaved down to a scale thickness.

I thinned down the leading and trailing edges of the sand skirts and the back end of the exhaust cover using a square file. The straps on the fuel drums were sanded smooth in preparation for the photo-etch ones included in the Extratech set. Unfortunately, I managed to lose one of the photo-etch buckles for the straps, and had to shave four sets off the Revell fuel drums. While working on the rear hull, I also added the Extratech grille covers, which are incredibly fine and a perfect fit. I shaved off the DML grab handles and replaced them with the tiny photo-etch parts; I have a new respect for Braille scale after fiddling with my tweezers and these minute parts! I added some very thin speaker wire for the headlights, and some punch and die discs formed the lenses.

Some Op Telic Challengers have a large tarp running across the glacis armour and roughly three-quarters of the length of the hull armour. To make this I rolled a thin sausage of Apoxie Sculpt. My Apoxie Sculpt work surface is a ceramic tile sprinkled with baby powder to stop it from sticking. Once I had a close diameter, I draped the roll of putty across the tank and cut it to fit. This was left to set up for about 10 minutes as I find it easier to work with after it's had a chance to toughen up. Using a dental pick, I pressed several vertical creases into the tarp – these are where I would later place tie-down straps. Then, using the same pick, I added horizontal creases running out from the tie-down locations. The straps were made by rolling the putty very thin and cutting it into strips using a straight razor. A brush dipped in water helped smooth out some of the rough areas. The sheet I had rolled thin was also used to make an air ID flag, which was draped over the turret and had folds worked into it using a fine probe. The rest of the work on the turret was equally straightforward with a precise parts fit and no putty required. Extratech brass was bent to form the GPMG cradle and ammo bin, but this was a bit like casting pearls before swine as the DML GPMG is easily the weakest part of the whole kit. The tips of the Smoke Grenade Launcher (SGL) barrels were moulded slightly out of round so as to give the impression they were rounded, I attached small discs to each end. An aerial made from sprue completed the turret.

Painting and weathering

The Op Telic Challengers were painted in what appears to be a semi-permanent tan colour, which leans towards yellow. It really did not seem to be the same shade of tan as the British forces used in Op Granby in 1991. The paint also wore very quickly, with large surfaces rubbing clear of tan and paint chips exposing the original green camouflage. Since I was modelling the tank after the battle for Basra Airfield, I decided to give the tan paint some fairly harsh weathering in keeping with the photos I'd seen of the Scots DG tanks.

I wanted to try an effect I'd read about in an old *Tamiya Modelling Magazine International* article by Robert Oehler. I was curious to see if the masking-chipping techniques he used in 1/35 scale could look as realistic in 1/72 scale. To begin, I basecoated the tank in a dark green mixture of Tamiya NATO Green and Field Grey. This had the advantage of doubling as a primer coat. Once the green was dry, I used a sharpened toothpick dipped in Humbrol latex mask, and began to mark out the areas where I wanted chips to appear. I had also tried using a 3M Scotch-brite pad to apply the masking fluid; however, this did not provide enough control in the small scale (it does work in 1/35 scale as I tried this technique again on the CrARRV later in the book).

I let the masking fluid dry for a day and then sprayed the tan coat, which was mixed using Tamiya Desert Yellow and Flat Yellow in a 3:1 ratio. Once dry, I used a toothpick to carefully pull off the mask. This was hard in that the spots where the latex had been applied were difficult to see under a coat of paint. A wooden toothpick was used to gently scrape away the latex, revealing the base green colour. I enhanced some of the scratches by painting more green and some Vallejo paint mixed to match the base colour with a 000 brush.

I masked off the tank and painted the CIP and air ID flag white, and then over-painted the CIP with orange. A mix of Vallejo brown and green was used to paint

An overall basecoat of Tamiya Olive Drab and Field Grey was applied, after which Humbrol latex mask was dabbed on with a sponge.

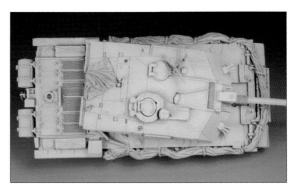

A mix of Tamiya Desert Yellow and Flat Yellow was sprayed over top. This colour is noticeably different from the tan colour used in Op Granby, and seemed to wear very easily.

The dried mask was gently removed with a toothpick. Try not to let the mask sit for more than two days otherwise it can be difficult to remove.

The kit provides decals for one option – a C Sqn, Scots DG, vehicle. The markings went on very well; however, the background of the Saltire is printed in black when it should be dark blue. Note that the point of the chevron always points to 9 o'clock.

the tarp, which seems to have a green tiger-stripe pattern printed on. The fire extinguishers were painted with olive drab and light blue to simulate the label and stencil. Once all the basic colours were applied, the decals went on. The DML decals are excellent and settled down well using Micro-Sol. A coat of Testors' Clear Flat Acryl sealed everything and prepared the model for weathering.

I began weathering by applying a thin wash of burnt sienna oil paint into the panel lines, crevasses, around bolt heads and the engine grilles. This was allowed to dry for a day and then I misted on a very thin coat of deck tan along the running gear. It's important to let each coat dry fully before reapplying, as it tends to dry more opaque and somewhat lighter than how it looks when it's freshly sprayed. I mixed up some Mig Pigments with some Tamiya thinner to match the dust colour, and dipped a short brush into the slurry. I flicked most of the mix off the brush into a paper towel, and once it was nearly devoid of the pastel solution, I flicked it carefully against front and rear mud flaps to simulate the dust and mud thrown up by the tracks. Some darker pastels were used to enhance the shadows and folds around the tarp and some black pastel was used on the engine exhaust.

Lastly, I added the glass for the episcopes by using coloured foil and some silver paint for the driving lights. While the silver paint was out, I drybrushed the GPMG to highlight some of the detail. I swapped the stretched sprue aerial with thin brass wire, and added extra aerials to the existing antenna mounts.

LEFT In addition to the green paint chips revealed by the mask, more chips were added using Humbrol 75 Green and a fine pointed brush.

BELOW Pastel chalks were dusted on in some of the deeper recesses.

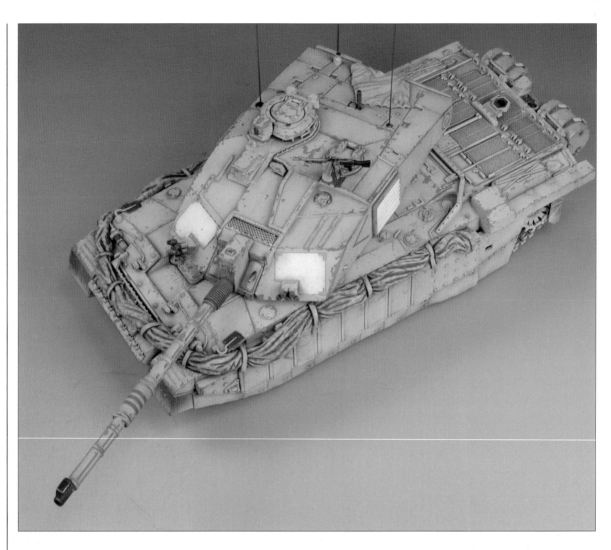

The small size of the Cr 2 meant some settings on the camera had to be adjusted. For these photos, I set the aperture at F10 and used a spot centre-weighted meter. To get the close-up photos I relied on the camera zoom instead of situating the lens close to the model, as this can block out the light.

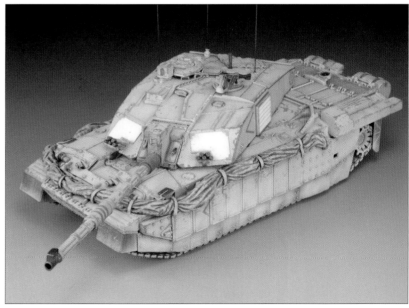

Challenger 1 Mk 3, 4th Armoured Brigade, Op Granby c.1991

Construction and photography by Graeme Davidson	
Finishing by Pat Johnston	
Degree of Difficulty:	★☆☆☆☆
Kit used:	*Revell Challenger 1 KFOR (3120).*
Additional detailing sets used:	*Extratech photo-etch set for Challenger 1 (72005), CMK Cr 1 Equipment Set (065), CMK Modern British Equipment (060), CMK Tent Packs (062), Apoxie Sculpt, Evergreen rod.*
Markings:	*Kit supplied.*
Paints:	*Tamiya Acrylics XF-59 Desert Yellow, XF-52 Flat Earth, XF-62 Olive Drab, XF-9 Hull Red, XF-69 NATO Black, XF-55 Deck Tan and XF-57 Buff; Vallejo 916 Sand Yellow, 950 Black and 847 Dark Sand; Testors' Chrome Silver; Winsor & Newton Raw Umber; Mig Pigments 023 Smoke and 027 Light Dust, and Rembrandt Raw Umber pastel chalk.*
References:	Jane's Armour and Artillery 2003, *Concord: 7505 Challenger 1 & 2, 2002* Op Granby: Desert Rats Armour and Transport in the Gulf War, *2006* Op Desert Sabre: The Desert Rats' Liberation of Kuwait.

Background

In October 1990, the British government moved the 7th Armoured Brigade from Germany to Saudi Arabia as part of Operation Granby, more commonly known by the coalition codename Desert Storm. Prior to crossing the line of departure on 24 February 1991, the 172 Challenger 1 Mk 3s of the 7th and 4th Armd Bdes were fitted with appliqué armour to the side skirts, explosive reactive armour to the glacis and extra fuel drums mounted on the rear hull. When Kuwait was recaptured some five days after H-Hour, the 1st (UK) Armoured Division had destroyed roughly 300 Iraqi tanks without losing a single Challenger.

Construction

After building the DML Challenger 2, I decided to include another 1/72-scale kit in the book for a short comparison. The Revell kit is a few years old, and is offered in both the SFOR and up-armoured KFOR and Gulf War versions. I was impressed by the level of detail on this kit, particularly around the engine deck. I decided to compare the moulding to the larger 1/35-scale kit from Tamiya and, as you can see, the Revell kit can really hold its own against its bigger brother.

There was not much to note during construction, other than you need to take care of the individual track links as they wrap around the idler wheels and drive sprockets. I chose to leave off the outer roadwheels until after they were painted as I find it is easier to paint the tracks while they are detached. The

LEFT AND BELOW The resin from CMK was crisply moulded, though the cam net did not 'rest' on the surface the whole way. These gaps were filled with Apoxie Sculpt (the grey areas), which was textured to match the resin item. The outer roadwheels were left off to make painting the track easier.

Revell fuel drums were replaced with scratch-built items as I could not sand the seam without destroying the ribs on the barrel. The new drum was made with a matching diameter tube capped with discs from the punch and die set and trimmed to fit. The ribs on the drums were made with very finely stretched sprue, to which a curl was imparted by dragging it across a straight edge. The same method of curling plastic was used for the .010in. strips that were used for the retaining straps. Attached to these strips were the handles shaved off from the original kit parts.

The CMK resin parts were added next, and the casting on these is outstanding, especially the soft stowage items. The rolled-up camouflage net was somewhat tricky to fit as I had inadvertently snapped it while detaching it from the runner. There were some gaps underneath it, but these were easily filled with Apoxie Sculpt. Once the Apoxie Sculpt had began to set, I jabbed it with a dental probe to match the texture of the CMK part. You can see where this was applied by the grey-coloured areas. I took some other CMK parts from the British tarp set and used these to fill out the stowage. The Extratech etch provides a fine mesh side and front stowage bins that you have to fold right the first time as repeated bending snaps the tiny brass tabs. Extratech also supplies two finely etched 20-litre fuel-can brackets; however, only one would fit on the Revell kit. I placed a CMK resin jug

External fuel drums were fashioned from tube styrene and the ridges were made using finely stretched sprue.

Posed next to the Tamiya kit, you can see that the side armour skirts on the 1/72-scale Challenger actually have better detail.

inside it. A spare wire reel was taken from another Challenger kit and detailed with stretched sprue spokes, a bent wire handle and fine wire wrapped around the reel. I took photographs of where I had mounted all the stowage as a reference. These were removed and had small holes drilled in the gluing surface into which I inserted small bits of sprue for painting handles.

Painting and weathering

The model was primed in Tamiya Flat Black and then painted in Desert Yellow, Buff and Sky Grey in a 4:1:1 ratio. This colour is lighter and redder than the Op Telic colour and I have included a few side-by-side photos to show how I interpreted the difference in these shades.

While it was drying, I painted the various stowage items shades of green and brown. They were given an oil-based wash and then drybrushed with Humbrol enamels. The straps were painted a medium brown colour from Vallejo. The long-range fuel drums were painted a mix of Tamiya Hull Red and Flat Black, as some of the Cr 1s in the Gulf were delivered in this colour. I picked out some other CMK bits in yellow and red to give some colour to the model – these choices were not based on any particular reference however.

The gun barrel shroud was painted a slightly darker tan than the tank, and the straps were picked out using a lighter version. These straps were framed by a thin wipe of dry Mig pastels. The cupola was not attached either, which made it easier to paint the optics. They were done with a coat of chrome silver followed by two coats of Tamiya Clear Green. The clear green pooled around the edges of the optics and dried darker, giving it a nice, though purely accidental, effect! The kit decals were next and went on using the Micro-Sol system with no difficulty. The only problem with the decals is that the kit supplied call sign '11B' is the commanding officer's tank of the 14th/20th Kings Hussars. That particular tank did not have the same external stowage as I had modelled, so the large side skirt, '11B' and 'Emperor' script were left off, with only the black Jerboa to identify this as a tank within the 4th Armd Bde. I used a sharpened green pencil crayon for the chipping as this gives a fairly restrained effect when compared to the liquid mask used in the previous chapter's Challenger 2. This was sealed under a coat of Testors' Clear Flat Acryl, which provides good 'bite' for the pigment powder application that I always do last. This pastel was brushed onto various shadows and then scrubbed away with a stiff brush, leaving just a slight shadow behind. The exhaust stain was made with Mig's black pastel and given a swept-back look.

The Cr 1 was painted much less yellow than the Cr 2 of Op Telic. The fuel drums were painted using Tamiya Hull Red.

The stowage was shaded using a wash-drybrush method. The cupola optics were first painted chrome silver and then given three coats of Tamiya Clear Green.

The real Cr 1s in the Gulf did not seem to exhibit the same degree of paint chipping as the Cr 2s in Op Telic. These paint chips were made with a sharp green pencil crayon.

The gun barrel was painted a slightly darker shade of khaki.

THIS PAGE AND OVERLEAF **The DML Cr 2 and Revell Cr 1** posed together show the colour variation and the similarities of the lower hull to good effect. Cr 1s also seem to have more external crew stowage than Cr 2s.

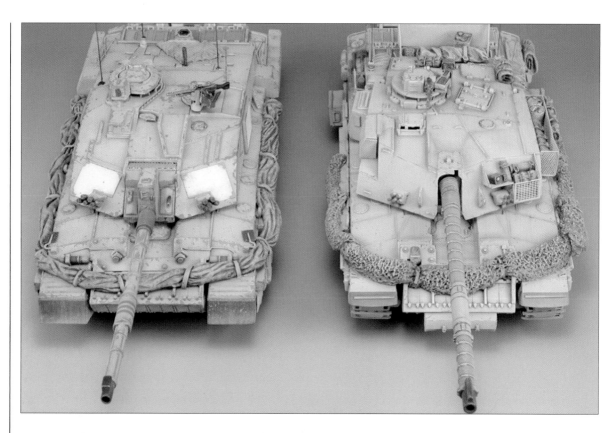

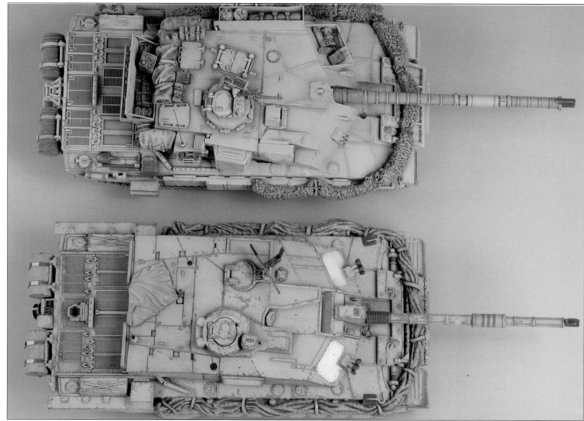

LEFT AND BELOW The Revell kit is very nice out of the box and, when detailed with photo-etch and resin, it can rival its 1/35-scale brother.

Desert Challenger 2, 1st Tank Regiment, Royal Army of Oman, Ex 'Saif Sareea II' c.2001

Degree of Difficulty:	★★★☆☆
Kit used:	*Tamiya Challenger 2 (Desertized) (35274).*
Additional detailing sets used:	*Friul Challenger 1 tracks (81), Extratech photo-etch for Challenger 2 (35023), Tamiya etched grilles (35277), Tamiya Allied Vehicles accessory set (35231), various Evergreen strip, sheet and rod, and colourized foil.*
Markings:	*Hand painted.*
Paints:	*Tamiya Acrylics XF-59 Desert Yellow, XF-69 NATO Black and XF-57 Buff; Gunze H372; Vallejo 916 Sand Yellow and 950 Black; Testors' Chrome Silver; Winsor & Newton Raw Umber; Mig Pigments 023 Smoke and Rembrandt Raw Umber pastel chalk.*
References:	*Jane's Armour and Artillery 2005, Concord: 7505 Challenger 1 & 2, Alvis Industry publications.*

Background

The Royal Army of Oman uses 38 Challenger 2s in its 1st Tank Regiment. These are modified from the British version as they are specifically designed to operate in temperatures up to 52°C. They retain the original engine and transmission, but the cooling system and airflow have been changed with larger radiators and fans being added. Note that this is not a Challenger 2E (Export) as has been reported in other publications – the Challenger 2E uses the German MTU 883 engine.

When I began this project, I was hoping that the Australian Army was going to select the Challenger 2E as its Leopard replacement. However, that competition was won by the US Abrams, which meant that at the time of writing, no army operates the Cr 2E.

The Omani version offered an interesting solution, in that it incorporates some features of the Challenger 2 and the 2E, and even retains the single-pin tracks of the Challenger 1. The manufacturer's brochures refer to this tank as Desert Challenger, which is confusing as the Tamiya kit is labelled Challenger 2 Desertized, though the two are quite different. I thought these modifications for a Desert Challenger would make for a more interesting take on the base Tamiya kit. As most of these changes are related to the hull, this chapter will concentrate on that area.

Construction

I began the conversion by cutting out the kit rear deck using a strand of dental floss. The deck was replaced by a large square of .040in. sheet. The rear hull plate was replaced by a blank sheet and trimmed to fit. Both sides of the hull and sponsons were replaced with plastic card, and the left side exhaust port was

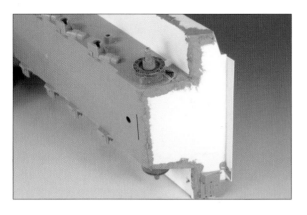

The Omani conversion begins with the filling in of the sponsons, the replacement of the hull sides and rear, and the cutting out of the kit engine deck. Note how the engine deck is cut oversize – it's easier to do this and trim back later than it is to try and make an exact cut.

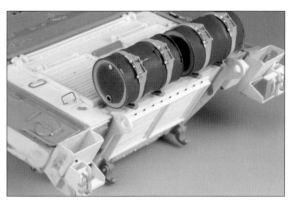

The fuel-strap buckles were shaved from the Tamiya kit and strips of masking tape over .010in. styrene were used for the actual straps.

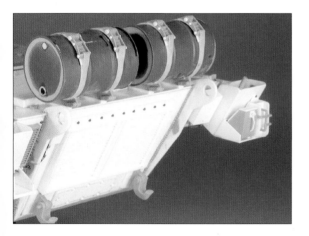

The large towing brackets were edged with a weld bead. The massive exhaust vents on the rear deck are simply strip styrene glued at a slight angle. This large vent necessitates relocating all the fittings that were on the original Cr 2 rear hull.

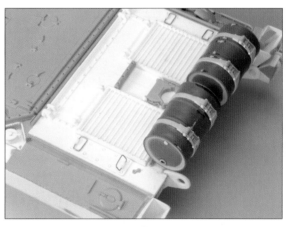

The multiple Cr 2 grilles were replaced by two large intakes designed to improve airflow around the engine. Lifting handles were fashioned from brass wire and hinges were made from styrene rod.

The left side exhaust is not present on RAO Challengers. In its place is a rectangular vent with an access hole covered with a pivoting cap.

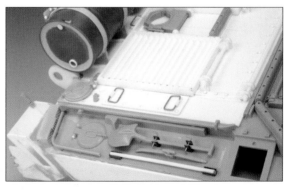

The right side retains the tool layout of the Challenger 1.

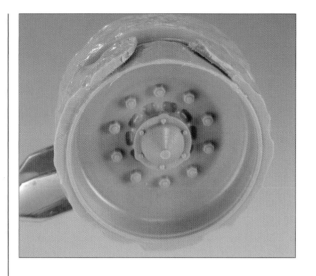

ABOVE I reckoned the stony desert of the Oman training area would wreak havoc on roadwheel rubber. A few wheels show the rubber peeling away in chunks. This effect is achieved using a cylindrical bit in a Dremel tool at very low speed.

ABOVE RIGHT The largest punch on the Historex set is a perfect match for the Thermal Imaging Sight. In this case, the coloured foil was placed behind the clear plastic to give it more depth.

RIGHT The TIS door with an actuating rod and the masking tape disc in place. The coaxial MG had each flange of the flash suppressor separated using dental floss as a saw.

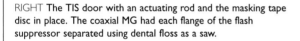

blanked off from below. I blocked off the sponsons as I was planning on displaying the tank without the side skirts installed. I prefer to get the big work out of the way first, before adding details to a particular spot. You can see from the pictures that I don't skimp on the putty when tackling this stage of a project, and not having small details glued on simplifies the sanding and smoothing process a great deal.

The main difference to the hull top is the two large square vents that replace the rectangular ones on the Challenger these are part of the engine cooling and ventilation modification required in the 40°C desert heat. These vents rest on a plate that sits proud of the engine deck, so if you want to just sand the deck smooth and glue on the new plate you could do that. I chose to remove the deck as I had a use for some of the grilles later on. The large intake vents had a number of angled strips inserted, but I lacked a clear photo of this grille so the actual number of slats is just a guess on my part. The gun cradle from the kit was placed in between the two vents and only the left side tool bin was attached. The right side bin area was replaced with a pioneer tool layout similar to that on the Challenger 1. The left exhaust vent is deleted on this version, and in its place is some sort of filler cap and vertical mesh grate. No thermal exhaust shield was fitted on any of the Omani Challengers that I saw. A fuel filler cap was salvaged from the kit, and some mesh screens were cut to fit over the vents, but these were not attached until a basecoat had been painted on. The final modification to the deck was the installation of the long-range fuel-drum brackets, which were made from customized kit parts.

Work on the rear hull plate began by building the two large vents that are centred on this plate. The installation of vents here required that all of the storage on the rear hull be relocated elsewhere on the tank. The turn signals were scratch built and reoriented vertically; while the kit-supplied brush guard was cut and modified to the Omani pattern. New water-jug brackets were built from .020in. plastic card and attached to the left and right side. Kit tow hooks were adapted to new mounting plates at the base of the rear, and an access panel was centred between them. A pair of lifting/recovery eyes was attached to the rear, these parts took several attempts to get right as there were a number of compound angles and they had to be a mirror image of each other. Each side of the bracket got a rod of stretched sprue that was textured with a heat gun to look like a weld bead. The last part was a rectangular vent mounted vertically between the left recovery bracket and water-can mount. This vent was carefully cut from the engine deck I removed earlier. The number of slats may not be an exact match, but it really looked the part.

A pair of 50-gallon drums was taken from the Tamiya Allied Vehicles accessory set. The Omani Challengers appear to use this standard drum as opposed to the British-style ones fitted to their tanks. I made filler lids from the punch and die set, using a varying diameter punch to produce the 'ring' lid on the end of the drum. Four straps of .010in. strip were curled and glued to the drums, while the kit ratcheting mechanisms were carefully shaved off the original part. I then glued eight strips of Tamiya tape and six bolt heads to each ratchet. The fuel drums were only tacked on with white glue as I planned to remove them for painting.

The swivel link (used with the recovery bars to form an A-frame) gets relocated to the hull side. Smaller intake vents were cut to fit from the Cr 2 deck.

ABOVE An M2 50-cal. MG was stolen from a Type 90 MBT, as it came with the correct brass and link collection baskets.

BELOW In profile, the RAO has an almost Soviet look to it, with the large high mount MG, slack tracks and deck-mounted fuel drums.

ABOVE The Friul track links were easy to work with, though after taking this photo I removed a link from each side.

BELOW The tow cable brackets came from the Trumpeter Cr 2 kit.

Moving to the right side of the hull, I began by making the attachment points for the side armour. These are a series of tabs with holes drilled in them; in between each tab is a black rubber strip, which I presume is to function as a gasket, keeping the dust from blowing up between the skirt and the hull. On the model, the tabs were simply .030in. strip cut into squares and drilled out. For the rubber strips I found a pack of semicircular Evergreen rods that fitted. The right side also has two spare track-link hangers (normally mounted on the rear hull of British Challengers) and a long rectangular vent. Again, this vent was salvaged from the engine deck, sanded square and edged with .010in. strip. Note that there is no tow cable mount on the right hull. The left side of the hull required the repositioning of the tow bar and swivel link attached to a triangular mounting plate. The circular tow cable mounting points and other tow cable hardware were taken from the kit and attached to the side, as were two U-shaped supports I had from a spare Trumpeter Challenger kit. Two vents cut from the kit deck (there wasn't much left of that deck by this point!) were also added.

The RAO decided to go with the single-pin track used on the Challenger 1. This was great, as it gave me an excuse to try out the new Friul tracks. It also meant adapting a Challenger 1 drive sprocket mount to the Cr 2 hull, which was pretty straightforward, just keeping in mind that the parts would be bearing some weight and had to be on straight. The rest of the running gear I decided to weather up thinking that the stony desert terrain would be harsh on the rubber. This was done with a rough file and a cylindrical bit (used like a router) in a Dremel tool. I tried to vary the wear and tear on the wheels to depict some that were freshly replaced and some that were on their last exercise. The Friul tracks (my first time using them) went together very easily. I started by pre-drilling the pin-holes, but found after a few links that this step was not required. Both runs took less than two hours to complete and are much better looking that the vinyl ones. You'll see in some of the photos that there is excessive sag; I fixed this during the photo shoot by removing a link. It's amazing how much extra tension taking only one link off can induce.

The front hull did not receive many extra details: just some wire for the headlights and a splash guard along the upper/lower hull join. The front mud flaps were shortened considerably, and thinned out from behind using a Dremel-tool cutting bit and a metal file.

The Tamiya kit comes moulded with a slight non-skid texture, but in my opinion it looks a little too restrained. For the sake of comparison and to satisfy my own curiosity, I decided to leave this model with the factory-moulded non-skid texture and apply a textured finish to another Challenger 2 appearing later in the book.

The turret only received minimal attention. The most obvious difference is replacing the MAG-58 GPMG with a pintle-mount M2 Browning .50 calibre. I should have scratch built the whole mount, but I realized the Type 90 JGSDF tank mount was virtually identical, so I adapted that to the Challenger. An A-frame mount and some etch and punch and die bits helped flesh out the detail on the gun.

For the Thermal Image Sight optics, I punched a disc of violet foil and attached that behind the clear plastic. The gun-sight door had an activation rod and brackets installed and a few bolt-head details. I cut the slots in the flash suppressor of the coaxial MG barrel using dental floss. That was tricky work, but I was able to rotate the part I messed up in towards the sighting box! Each of the turret storage-bin latches were boxed in and a small T-handle was installed for each one.

Painting and weathering

I masked off the optics, removed the tracks and fuel drums, and began to paint. I only had a few colour pictures of the RAO Cr 2 and the colours seemed to vary in each one. After basecoating in flat black, I initially painted the green and tan

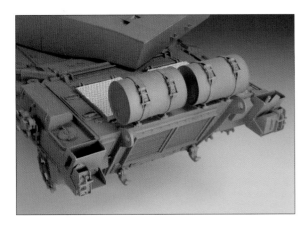

After priming in flat black, the aluminium mesh screens could be attached to the radiator screens.

My initial colour selection was based on a photo of an RAO Challenger painted in a buff and field green pattern.

Subsequent photos showed the tan to be a more orange shade, so I painted over the buff with Tamiya Desert Yellow.

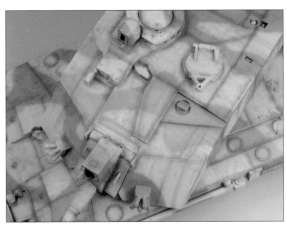

ABOVE AND BELOW LEFT Next I added black streaks and shadows, followed by faded areas made with thinned lighter versions of the base colour.

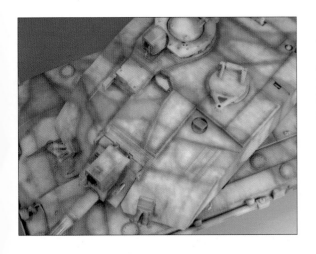

This was oversprayed with the pure base colour, highly diluted. In this picture two coats have been applied, but the effect is still too strong.

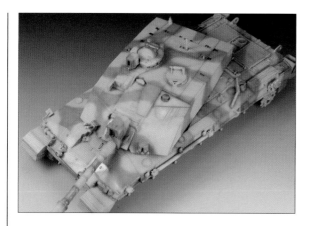

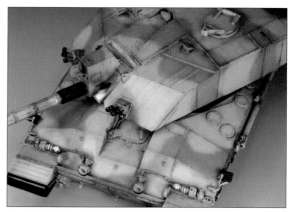

After four coats, the paint has a variety of tonal differences without looking too contrived.

After letting the decals dry, an oil paint wash was used in localized areas. Although the model looks very dark at this point, the subsequent flat coats lightened the paint considerably.

The various tools were brush-painted using Vallejo colours – this has got to be the best brushing acrylic I have ever used.

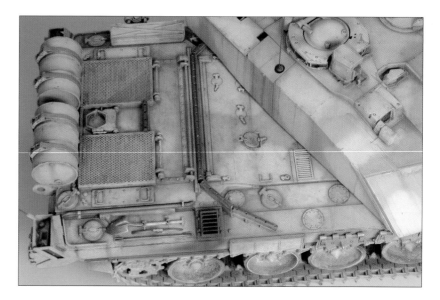

It's safe to remove the masking tape at this point. The circular sight above the main gun looks great under the clear plastic, though the rest of the optics are still a bit too bright for my liking.

Roadwheel mud was made from pastel chalk sifted on to the wheel dish and wetted with Tamiya thinner.

ABOVE AND BELOW LEFT A dirty black-brown mix was used for the exhaust staining while rust and brown pigments were used on the spare track links.

Grief 4mm lenses were placed on the headlights using white glue.

The rubber on the track pads was simply 'painted' by a finger dipped in Mig Black Pigment and then sealed with flat acryl.

camouflage pattern based on one photo that showed a very pale tan; however, this pale sand colour was too far off from the other pictures I had that showed a more orangey-tan colour. Furthermore, the Gunze Green used looked too dark. I decided to repaint the vehicle with a better shade of tan, this time using Tamiya Desert Yellow. This shade was a better compromise and, interestingly, the darker tan colour had the effect of making the green bands appear lighter. I used a Tamiya SF airbrush to obtain a fairly tight demarcation based on the photos I had.

Once the basic pattern was sprayed I immediately loaded up the airbrush with some watery black-brown, which was sprayed along panel lines and low points, as well as used for some random streaking. This is the first step in varying the colour finish as I find if the pure colours are left on, the finish is a bit stark. The next step is to offset the black with some lightened mixes of the base colours. These are sprayed on the upper surfaces that would be more prone to sun fading than the vertical sections. The effect at this point is exaggerated and not very realistic. To bring it back a notch, I mixed very thin, near water-like colour mixes of the pure base colour. These 'toner' coats were then gradually reapplied, blending in with the dark streaks and pale fading with each successive coat. In this case, I made three applications of the toner until I was happy with the variety in the finish. At this point I took an in-progress photo and realized that much of the subtle fading was being 'washed out' by the bright photo lights. It made me wonder if I should try and exaggerate the finish so it would show in the book, and look odd in real life? I decided to add a dark oil-paint wash to pick up some of the surface detail, and also made a mental note to 'go heavy' on the airbrush effects for the next model to see if it would photograph differently (see the chapter on the Falcon 2 for comparison). I then painted the various detail bits such as fire extinguishers, rubber cushions and the Arabic numerals for the registration plate.

I sprayed on a couple of coats of Polly-S Flat, which reminds me of the old Aeromaster acrylic flat coat. It's great stuff, though you do need to clean the airbrush right away as it leaves a cloudy film on the nozzle and in the paint cup.

Setting aside the model for a night, I worked on weathering the Friul tracks. I put these in a small tub and poured some Blacken-It solution on them. This stuff chemically reacts with the tracks much the same as gun blue for firearms. It does stink, and I wore latex gloves and safety goggles while handling it. The tracks sit in the liquid for about 15 minutes; all the while I use an old stiff-bristled paintbrush to work the solution in between all the links. Once the liquid turns a murky brown, it appears to stop working, and I removed the tracks, laying them out on a paper towel. Once dry, I added a thin mix of brown pigments, let that dry, and applied an oil wash. I set them aside for a night and then dipped my finger into some back pigments to colour the track pads and the roadwheel contact patch.

I had decided early on with the chewed-up roadwheels that I would depict this tank as being put through its paces, perhaps at the conclusion of an Ex 'Saif Sareea' field training exercise. That meant it would need to be mucked up a bit, which was accomplished with ground pastels sprinkled on the roadwheels and lower hull, which had been pre-wetted with Tamiya thinner. Just apply the thinner with a quick wipe – if you start to work it into the surface, it will eat through the paint. Once the pastel mud was dry, I added some discolouration with darker pastels and some paint. This has the effect of looking like wet mud, or grease from the hub seals.

I airbrushed a quick streak of flat black for the exhaust port and covered that again with a mix of black and light grey pigments. While the black was in the brush, I painted the MG and later drybrushed it silver.

Lastly, I made a few paint chips with a 2B pencil, coated the model with a few blasts of XF Buff, peeled off the tape masks covering the optics and added some brass wire antennas.

Challenger Armoured Repair & Recovery Vehicle, 32 Regt RE, Op Grapple, United Nations Protection Force, Bosnia-Herzegovina c.1995

Construction and photography by Graeme Davidson	
Finishing by Pat Johnston	
Degree of Difficulty:	★★★☆☆
Kit used:	*Accurate Armour CrARRV (C024), Tamiya Challenger 1 (lower hull) (35154).*
Additional detailing sets used:	*Accurate Armour 5-gal oil drums (017), 7.62mm GPMG ammo boxes (016), copper wire.*
Markings:	*Kit supplied, Archer UNPROFOR Markings (35177).*
Paints:	*Tamiya XF-62 Olive Drab, XF-67 NATO Green, XF-2 Flat White, XF-69 NATO Black and XF-57 Buff; Vallejo 950 Black and 847 Dark Sand; Mig Pigments 33 Dark Mud.*
References:	Jane's Military Vehicles and Logistics 2005, UN Peacekeeper Recognition Guide Volume 1, *1998 edition.*

Background

The British Army operates some 81 Challenger ARRVs to support the Challenger fleet, as well as other heavy vehicles such as the AVRE and AVLB. Unofficially known as the Rhino, the CrARRV can lift a Challenger 1 or 2 powerpack with its 6,500kg crane, or tow vehicles weighing up to 68 tons. The large dozer blade can also be used as an earth anchor when winching.

While it's not a tank, I thought the CrARRV would make an interesting addition to this book as they play an important role in the armoured regiments. When I first found out that the CrARRVs were deployed on UNPROFOR, I started to think how much fun it would be to chip and weather this massive vehicle. However, here is the disclaimer: I only saw two photos of the CrARRV in United Nations' White, and both appeared to be taken at the dock as they disembarked from the RO-RO transport ship. As such, they were finished in factory-fresh pristine gloss white ... but that's no fun to paint! The weathering used in this chapter is based on other white-painted British UNPROFOR vehicles such as Warriors and Combat Engineer Tractors.

Construction

The AA kit requires you to use the lower hull and running gear from the Tamiya Challenger 1. I think there are online hobby shops that will cater to orders of specific sprues, so that might be a way to go about getting the parts required for this conversion. I got a low-priced Cr 1 from eBay, so I didn't feel too bad about chucking 75 per cent of an otherwise perfectly fine kit away.

The AA kit is well cast and appears to have been recently updated as the one I bought had less white metal parts than other AA CrARRVs that I have seen. My preference is to work in resin over white metal, so this is a good change. I made only a few changes to the kit, namely replacing the moulded-open storage bins with ones made from plastic card and stainless-steel mesh, adding hydraulic lines made from copper wire and a small storage bin from AA's UK Tank storage bins. AA also provides brass side skirts; however, I decided to make mine out of styrene and copper wire. Some water and fuel cans were taken from the Tamiya Challenger and I was able to make some spare Challenger wheels from a leftover hull. These were gently sanded against a block until the centre hub fell out, then a drill bit the same diameter as the lug nuts was used to make a ring of holes around the hub. Some items from AA's British Bergens and Rucksacks help complete the storage. All of the major subassemblies were left off to make painting easier. The reason I've rated this a three-star as opposed to two-star difficulty level is due to the painting and weathering, which is a bit more involved than usual, otherwise this is a great beginner-level resin conversion.

Painting and weathering

The first step in this process was to gather as many photos of UNPROFOR AFVs that I could find. *The Peacekeeper Recognition Guide* has many such pictures, and it was used as my primary reference for weathering.

I mixed up a batch of British green from Tamiya Olive Drab, NATO Green and Field Grey. I wasn't too fussy about the colour as it was only going to be showing through in chips. I did, however, make up enough of the mix so that I could add paint chips after spraying, and they would still be the same colour as the base.

This base green was applied in two coats over the whole kit; it was then clear-coated with Humbrol Matt Varnish for extra strength. I used some Humbrol latex mask and tore up a 3M Scotch-Brite green scouring pad and dipped it in the liquid mask. I then dabbed the pad on the edges and high points of the vehicle, and especially around the dozer blade. This was allowed to dry for a day (don't let the mask dry for more than two days or it can be hard to remove). Next I airbrushed on a coat of Tamiya Flat White. Yes, UN vehicles seem to have been painted in gloss white, but I find that gloss just doesn't look 'right' on a model. Once the paint was dry, I started peeling off the latex mask. Overall, the effect looked okay, but not what I had envisioned. In short, it looked more like someone had removed latex mask than a really worn and chipped finish.

The next step was to take the Scotch-Brite pad and dip it in the base green colour. This was then dabbed against a paper towel until almost devoid of paint. Like dry-sponging instead of drybrushing. Moving to the model, I gently dabbed the pad around the previously chipped areas, rotating and varying the position of my hand so as to not get a uniform series of stamped chips. After this stage, the finish was looking much better, but I felt it could still be enhanced by using a 00 brush and carefully painting on some scratches and playing 'connect the dots' with some of the more heavily worn areas. This was the effect I was looking for and, though somewhat time consuming, I think the result was worth it.

With the chips out of the way, I painted the detail items. The optical glass was done in silver with two coats of Tamiya Clear Green and, for some colour, I painted the vice a medium blue and then picked out the extinguishers in red. For markings, I used a mix of the AA kit decals and the Archer UN markings.

A thin oil wash (much thinner than usual due to it going over a white surface) was flowed into panel joins and around bolt heads. A mist of flat brown and deck tan was hazed along the side skirts and a dark brown/black mix was sprayed over the exhaust. The dozer blade got a wipe along the scraping edge using ground-up pencil lead and my Mk 1 finger. A coat of clear acryl was sprayed over everything, and then I painted the lights gloss silver, red and orange, and made streaks using Mig Pigments. Rust-coloured pigments were mixed with Tamiya thinner and washed into the front winch pulleys, flowed along some of the cables and allowed to pool in the recesses. The cables were then given a wipe of graphite and polished with a cotton bud.

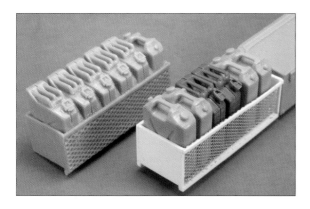

ABOVE, ABOVE RIGHT AND BELOW LEFT The Accurate Armour CrARRV does not need much straight from the box. I tweaked the two storage bins, replacing them with steel mesh and styrene, and used a variety of stowage from Tamiya, Accurate Armour and Verlinden to fill up the bins.

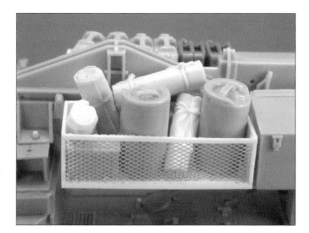

Copper wire for hydraulic hoses. I added extra slack to the lines since all the pistons are compressed ... except the lines are attached to a cylinder that remains at more or less a fixed distance.

Certain parts and subassemblies were left unattached to make painting and weathering easier.

AA even includes some heavy recovery chain to drape over the rear hangers.

Braided copper wire from Karaya is used for the winch cable.

BELOW The completed model before painting.

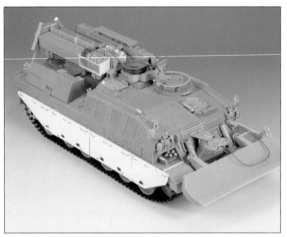

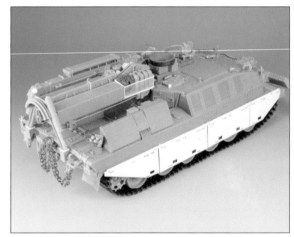

ABOVE, ABOVE RIGHT AND BELOW LEFT After painting the kit in British green, a Scotch-Brite pad was used to dab Humbrol liquid mask along areas subjected to high wear and traffic. After this, the model was then painted white and further paint chips were added with a fine brush. The dozer blade would see the most wear, and it is weathered correspondingly.

The tow chains got a liquid pigment coating of rust and then a wipe with some pencil lead to simulate worn metal.

Extra chipping was added to the edges of the crane.

Roadwheels came from a spare Challenger kit, and seemed to be a logical choice for stowage on an ARRV.

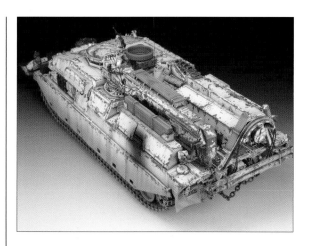

Flat earth mixed with buff was sprayed along the lower hull for a light accumulation of dirt on a vehicle that did not venture off road much due to the anti-tank mine threat.

ABOVE AND BELOW LEFT A black oil paint wash was flowed into the engine deck grilles while black acrylic was used for the exhaust staining. Archer fine transfers were used for the 'UN' stencils.

AA toolbox attached to the fender as improvised storage.

The crew commander's optics were painted silver followed by three coats of Tamiya Clear Green. The GPMG was painted black and the metal parts were drybrushed chrome silver.

The front edge of the dozer blade got a wipe with powdered pencil lead and was then buffed with a paper towel.

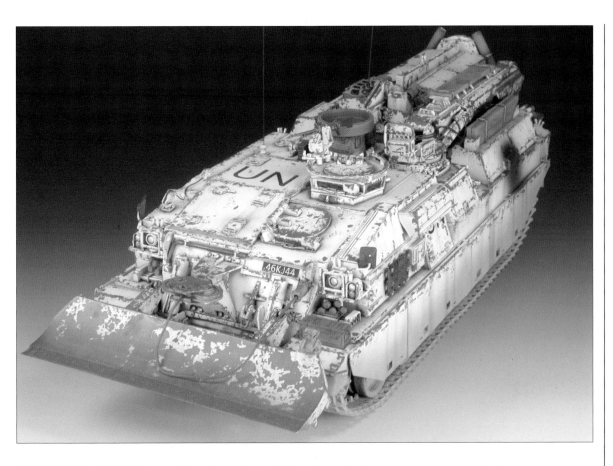

THIS PAGE AND OVERLEAF A coat of clear flat acrylic from Polly-S paints seals the finish and helps guard against fingerprints.

Challenger 2, Royal Dragoon Guards, Op Telic c.2005

Degree of Difficulty:	★★★☆☆
Kit used:	*Tamiya Challenger 2 (Desertized) (35274)*
Additional detailing sets used:	*Accurate Armour stand-off armour (C086), Extratech photo-etch for Challenger 2 (35023), 3mm Grief lenses.*
Markings:	*Kit supplied, hand painted.*
Paints:	*Tamiya XF-59 Desert Yellow, XF-26 Deep Green, XF-57 Buff, XF-1 Flat Black and XF-2 Flat White; Vallejo 916 Sand Yellow, 950 Black and 847 Dark Sand; Testors' Chrome Silver; Winsor and Newton Raw Umber; Mig Pigments 023 Smoke and Rembrandt Raw Umber pastel chalk.*
References:	*Jane's Armour and Artillery 2003, Concord 7505 Challenger 1 & 2, photos via Simon Dunstan to be published in Osprey New Vanguard 112: Challenger 2 MBT.*

Background

After the initial invasion of Iraq shifted from a conventional to a guerrilla war, many coalition vehicles responded to the increased threat of Rocket Propelled Grenade (RPG) attacks in complex terrain by modifying their armour. I believe the first vehicle to wear bar armour in Iraq was the US Stryker; however, other vehicles, such as the Australian LAV-25 as well as the British Warrior and Challenger, soon began to follow suit. For the Challenger, this meant adding extra Chobham armour to the turret sides and slat armour around the rear and sides of the hull and turret. This spaced armour is designed to interfere with shaped-charge warheads by causing premature detonation and disrupting the penetrating stream of metal.

Construction

In this case, the first step of the construction process involved painting, since I had decided to enhance the non-skid texture. There are a couple of techniques that can be used for this. Some involve painting an adhesive onto the plastic and coating it with fine grit, others use highly thinned putty spattered on via an airbrush. I wanted to try a technique shown to me by Jim Carswell that uses a rattle can texture paint. In this case, the product is known as Rustoleum Texture Finish. It comes in a variety of metallic colours; I happened to have a can of nickel silver already in the garage so I used that. Before spraying I had to mask off the areas that would not get the non-skid texture.

The first picture gives a good idea where to mask, but note that I should have not masked the centre section of the circular panels or the outer corners of the engine deck. Also, to apply the texture to the turret, I reckoned it would be easier once it was partially assembled. The only deviation from the instructions here was to box in the turret storage bin-handle recesses and fill the episcopes with plastic card. For a bit of variation, I took a spherical Dremel bit and made the

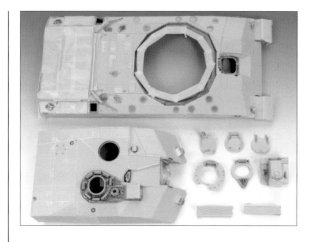

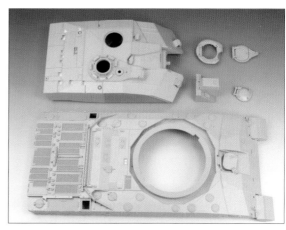

Prior to spraying the non-skid surface, certain areas need to be masked off using either Tamiya tape or liquid mask.

A few quick passes with the Rustoleum Texture spray and the non-skid was done. Leave the tape on for 24 hours to let the texture spray reach a hardness level where it can be handled.

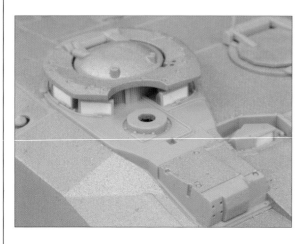

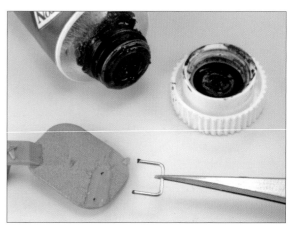

The optical inserts were filled with styrene so I could try out a different technique on the optics.

A good trick for ensuring you drill holes in the correct place: use a dab of oil paint on the ends of the part and it acts like a stamp.

An X-Acto chisel blade was reshaped with the Dremel tool to get into tight places, like these moulded-on engine deck handles.

All the deck handles were replaced with copper wire and the forward screens had Tamiya etched grilles added. These really ought to be included with the kit and not purchased separately.

SGL caps concave instead of convex. Note that the forward side of the turret also has the non-skid applied for some reason, perhaps to reduce the reflectivity of that area? Usually, it is only applied to horizontal walking surfaces. Masking the large areas was basically monkey work consisting of cutting strips of tape, while for the round areas, small spots, and complex shapes I found Humbrol Liquid Mask to be a better choice.

After shaking the spray can for a good couple of minutes, I held it about 18in. from the model and did one very quick, very light pass just to test it. It didn't dissolve the plastic or melt any parts, so I proceeded with another two light coats covering the whole model. The stuff reaches full strength after curing for a day, so I just left it to dry. The texture is really nice, it has a very 'in scale' look to it. The only complaint I have, and this is really nit picking, is that the texture is just a bit too uniform. I removed the masking tape and latex mask and thought the effect to be pretty nice, though I wondered if it would show up in the photographs under a coat of paint.

There were no dramas with the rest of the Tamiya build. I fashioned a micro-chisel out of an old X-Acto blade using a grinding wheel in the Dremel. This narrow chisel edge was used to remove the moulded-on engine deck handles, which were replaced with bent copper wire. Pat Johnston passed a handy trick on to me – using oil paint to mark the ends of the bent wire. The wire is then placed in position on the hull, and the oil paint transfers from the copper to the plastic. This gives a precise indication where to drill the holes for the handles. While working on the engine deck, I also added some hinge details and some Tamiya etched screens. The front hull got the usual headlight wires and I installed some empty fire extinguisher brackets from the Extratech set. The ROMOR (explosive reactive armour) frame had the top attachment bolts drilled out. This was to insert a styrene rod and bolt head combination, to give the impression it is actually attached to the front hull brackets.

Virtually the entire kit was built before delving into the mass of photo-etch and resin that comprises the AA conversion. The first thing I noticed about this conversion was the quality of the instructions. Sometimes I have a devil of a time figuring out AA's directions, but their new approach to picture-driven directions is much appreciated. I started with the larger resin bits – which initially had me wondering at first why AA had bothered to cast new side armour when the Tamiya parts looked fine to me. Looking closer, I eventually noticed that this version of the Challenger has different side armour from the Tamiya kit – there are nine rectangular panels versus seven. I added the copper wire tow cable, but only for the in-progress photos – I did not glue it to the cable ends as this allowed me to remove it and paint separately.

The next task was to assemble the photo-etch slats and rods. These go together quite well, but I have to emphasize that you need to take your time and line everything up, in which case you'll be rewarded with a perfectly fitting armour section. The only one I rushed was the only one that did not turn out square. I used CA glue to assemble the frames, though the soldering wizards may want to try using that method for extra strength. I found the frames were prone to popping if handled too much – nothing a little more CA wouldn't fix, but after a while it does tend to blob up in the joins.

The rest of the mounting hardware goes on without a problem, though some of the scoring lines on which you must bend the photo-etch are a bit wide. This can mean that if you don't make the 90-degree bend in the right spot, over the course of four bends on a part the error budget can be exceeded, resulting in a part that is out of square. However, once it is hidden under the slat armour panels, the mistake is barely noticeable.

I left the bar sections off as I imagined trying to paint the kit with them attached would be very difficult. Reattaching them after painting required some touch ups, but since this kit was going to be a uniform dark green, I wasn't worried about not being able to match the paint.

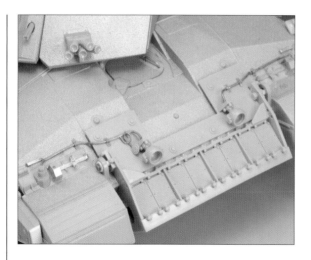

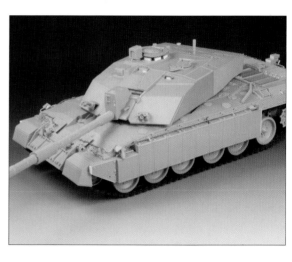

Copper wire provides the conduit for the lights and horn while the extinguisher mount is from an Extratech photo-etch set.

The Accurate Armour side panels are fitted – note that these are a different configuration from the Tamiya kit parts.

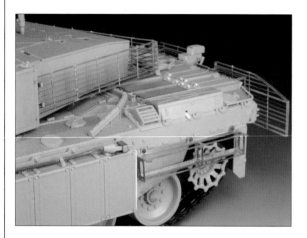

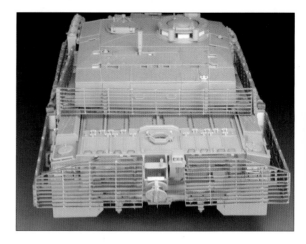

ABOVE MIDDLE LEFT AND RIGHT, ABOVE LEFT AND RIGHT Test-fitting the slat armour required a delicate touch. I used CA glue to assemble these, but I think solder would be a better route. The AA instructions are pretty clear, but I found I had to consult some reference photos to figure out the rear turret mounts. Before painting the brass, I removed it from the kit and gave it several coats of automotive primer. The small nubs protruding from the top and bottom slats were ground almost completely down with a Dremel. You don't want it to be perfectly flush as the real armour has these small bumps.

About the paint – one thing I have noticed on the pictures of this tank in Iraq is that the green colour seems to be different from the shade used in the UK. It is more a forest green colour, very similar in appearance to the US Strykers. I am only guessing, but perhaps the desert tan was painted over using US paint stocks in theatre? On some of the Iraq Challengers, the ROMOR armour frame on the glacis is still desert tan, as is the GPMG mount, though that varies.

Painting and weathering

I began by priming all the photo-etch with auto body primer. As it's designed to do, this primer helps show flaws in the surface, which there were, unfortunately, a fair amount of, mostly blobs of glue. I scraped these back with an X-Acto blade, polished them with a rubber and grit bit in the Dremel, and re-sprayed with primer.

Then I painted the whole kit and the photo-etch parts with Tamiya NATO Black. I then prepared a green mix using Tamiya Deep Green, which seemed a good match to the colour photos I'd seen of tanks taken in theatre. It might just be a trick of the light, but the shade of green used to repaint the tan tanks used in the early stages of Op Telic looks a lot more 'green' than the camouflaged Challengers back in Europe. I didn't see much evidence of chipping so I was going to limit my weathering to some paint fading and natural elements such as dust, mud, and a light rust for the tracks.

I also thought I'd try a different style of finishing new to me. In chatting with modeller friends on www.missing-lynx.com, I've noted that there is a whole spectrum of weathering styles in vogue. At one end, there is the highly stylized finishes, commonly referred to as 'artistic' (for want of a better term), and at the other end we've labelled the finish as 'realistic'. I tend to gravitate towards a more stylized weathering, but this time I wanted to experiment with a more 'realistic' finish.

So, not really knowing how to go about this, but with an idea of what I wanted the end result to look like, I began painting. I've included all the steps here – including my mistakes along the way, and the steps that ultimately proved unnecessary.

I began by spraying the optics titanium silver, clear red and clear blue, and painting the tail lights clear red and clear orange. After a couple of coats these were masked off. First up was a coat of the deep green, which I found to be a decent match – though when photographed against a blue background it seemed more 'green' than in real life.

The next stage was to paint the dark and light shades as described in the RAO Challenger chapter. A toner coat of thinned deep green muted this. I painted some of the details at this point, such as the white gun-barrel ID bands, the tan frame for the ERA, the metallic bolt heads and washers, and all the other 'black bits' as I'd started calling them by this point.

Now here is where the weathering process deviated from what I am used to. Rather than flow a dark wash into the recesses, I wanted to depict the accumulation of dust in the panel lines and other recessed areas. I knew this would look odd, as it's pretty rare to see a dark green tank in a desert environment, so there would be a fair amount of contrast.

I began by making a water-based pastel wash from Mig sand pigments. This was flowed on in all the places I'd normally do a dark wash, putting extra into the nooks where I reckoned more dust would collect. I let this dry, and it looked horrible! It was far too overdone, so I took a short bristled brush, and carefully 'scrubbed' back the dried pastel to lessen the effect. This looked a bit better, but the contrast was still too high, and there was something wrong with the look that I couldn't yet put my finger on. I wondered if the dust was too yellow, and so I prepared another wash, only instead of pastels, this time I used oil paints: white, yellow ochre and a dab of black. This made a more grey/tan mix, and I flowed this directly over the yellow-tan pastel wash. However, it was

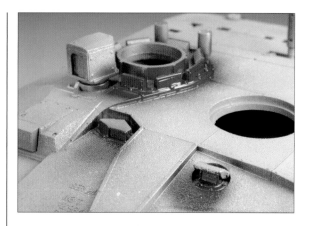

The optics were first painted Tamiya Titanium Silver, and then Clear Red and Clear Blue was mixed and sprayed on in three coats. The colour in real life is a dark cherry red, but for some reason, the digital camera is showing this colour a much brighter shade.

Tamiya Deep Green is a decent match for the repainted Op Telic Challengers.

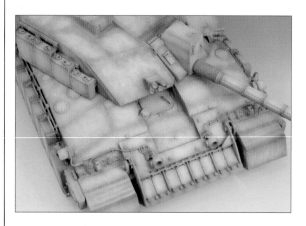

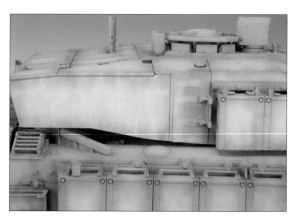

ABOVE AND ABOVE RIGHT Here are the shading and the lightening steps combined. The close-up photo shows the random nature of the shading and fading.

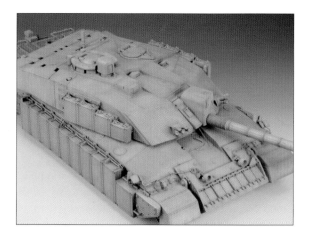

ABOVE AND ABOVE RIGHT After a thinned coat of the base colour (deep green and thinner in a 1:10 ratio) the garish shading

is toned down. Even with multiple coats of paint, the non-skid texture is still visible.

Vallejo paints were used for the details. A few Challengers still had tan-painted parts, namely the ROMOR armour frames and the GPPMG mounts.

ABOVE AND BELOW LEFT This is not what I wanted – the pastel wash was difficult to control as I tried to replicate the effect of lighter dust accumulating on a dark vehicle.

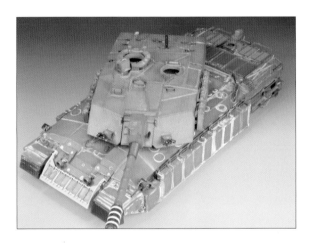

ABOVE AND BELOW LEFT This wash was literally scrubbed back using a short-bristled brush and running water. The effect looked better, but was still not what I had in mind. It was around this time that I figured out the dust was too yellow.

The bar armour was attached at this point so as to prevent the weathering of the tank from looking too different, Front and rear roadwheels were attached to prevent the delicate rear hanging armour from contacting the ground.

ABOVE A greyish-tan mixture was fed through the airbrush and applied over the yellow-tan areas. Grey oil paints were also applied in a localized manner. I thought this was a marginal improvement and decided to try the pastel trick again.

ABOVE RIGHT AND RIGHT This time, I mixed grey and tan pastels with water and applied it over the whole model. While wet, a streaking pattern was achieved by dragging a nearly dry brush dipped in Tamiya thinners along vertical parts. Darker brown pastel was flicked onto the rear areas of the side armour to show a watery mud spray.

still not the effect I was going for. At this time, I decided to fit the slat armour, as I did not want the weathering to progress too far on the tank and then have the bar armour look brand new.

I practically repainted the tank using four thinned toner coats right over the dust wash. After that, I loaded the airbrush with some thinned grey acrylics, which I tried to 'spray' on in a wash pattern, but again, the effect was really not where I wanted it to be! This was starting to get a little frustrating, though with some encouragement from some fellow modellers I gave it another shot.

The next method worked for me, and basically negated every step after painting the model in its green basecoat! I mixed up a wash of tan and raw umber (making a greyish brown colour) of pastel chalks with water, and with a broad brush, flooded the entire surface of the model. I dried this with a hair dryer and scrubbed away the spots I thought were too dirty, while avoiding areas of high foot traffic such as around the crew cupolas. The muddy streaks were made by dipping a one-quarter inch flat brush in Tamiya thinner and then dabbing it against a paper towel until it was almost dry. This was then whisked against the side armour parts, creating a clean streak effect. Near the rear of the tank, I mixed a slightly thicker pastel slurry and used a small brush to flick droplets of the pigment in a mud-spray pattern. This process was repeated on the front and rear hulls. Finally, a thin coat of buff was sprayed at an upwards angle along each edge of the lower hull.

Extra pastel dust was stippled around the loader's and commander's hatches to show the mud that would scrape off their boots on the non-skid surface. The edges of the top hull were just wiped back with a soft cloth moistened with water, the rationale being that dust would not accumulate on high points and edges.

LEFT AND BELOW The bar armour was mucked up using the same pastel colour, but in a slightly thicker mix. After the pastels were applied, a thin mix of buff and deck tan was sprayed along the lower hull, pointing from the ground up.

The GPMG mount was left in tan, and shows the increased chipping associated with that type of paint. The Union flag on the commander's sight is a non-standard marking.

RIGHT, BELOW AND OPPOSITE
After applying the pigment wash, some 3mm MV lenses were glued into the driving light housings. The pigments are not sealed by any clear coat, as this can sometimes mute the effect. As such, the kit must be carefully handled to avoid leaving fingerprints.

Falcon 2 AB9C5, 7th Tank Battalion, 99th Armoured Brigade, Jordanian Army

Degree of Difficulty:	★★★★☆
Kit used:	*Tamiya Challenger 1 (lower hull) (35154).*
Additional detailing sets used:	*Modelpoint L55 120mm gun (3559-2), Grief 2.5mm lenses.*
Markings:	*Hand painted.*
Paints:	*Gunze Acrylics H336 Hemp, H372 FS 34227, H37 Wood Brown and H340 FS 34097; Tamiya XF-57 Buff, XF-1 Flat Black, XF-2 Flat White, XF-3 Flat Yellow, XF-7 Flat Red and X-27 Clear Red; Vallejo 950 Black; Testors' Chrome Silver; Winsor & Newton Raw Umber; Mig Pigments 023 Smoke; and Rembrandt Raw Umber pastel chalk.*
References:	*Jane's Armour and Artillery 2005, www.kaddb.com.*

Background

For the last chapter in this book, I thought I'd have a little fun and build one of the lesser-known Challengers, the Jordanian Falcon 2. Jordan has been using the Al Hussein (Challenger 1) since 1999, and some four dozen tanks equip the 7th Bn of the 99th Armd Bde. The Falcon turret is a project by the King Abdullah II Design Bureau (KADDB) of Jordan with partnership from South African, Swiss and UK firms. The latest version of this turret, the Falcon 2, is mounted on a Challenger 1 hull. The turret uses a Ruag 120mm smoothbore as opposed to the Royal Ordnance rifled barrel, and the crew is located down inside the hull while the human loader has been replaced with a ten-round autoloader located in the rear of the turret. When I first saw pictures of this tank at an arms trade show, I knew I had to build it! Unfortunately, getting reference photos was hard, and scale drawings impossible. But sometimes you have to build with what you've got, and I had about 15 photos that I could use to extrapolate the basic dimensions of the turret from since I had a known measurement in the form of the Tamiya Challenger 1 hull to compare it to. I also decided that I would like to build this as an 'in service' tank as opposed to the company demonstrator prototype.

Construction

I began by sketching an outline on some card paper and holding it above the kit hull while comparing it to the various photos. I must have drawn a dozen of these before I had a profile that matched the pictures. This process was repeated for the other sides, and once satisfied, I began to cut some plastic. This plastic is regular .040in. plastic card that has been coloured yellow. The .040in. card has a good sturdy thickness that is ideal for making basic structural shapes. If you haven't yet noticed I am a really sloppy builder! I rarely, if ever, try to cut

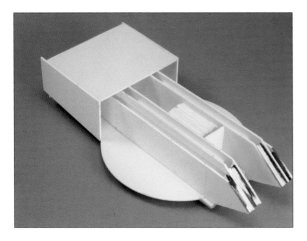

The rough frame of the Falcon turret is built using sturdy .040in. styrene.

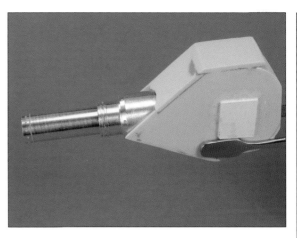

Test-fitting the 120mm L55 cannon into the mantlet.

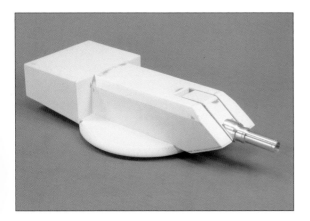

The rough shape of the turret has to be right before any detail work begins. I think I got it right on the third try!

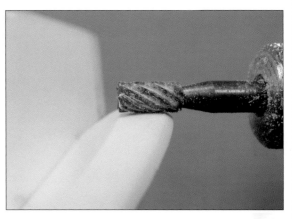

The cylinder bit roughly shapes the bevel on the base of the turret. This was a time for 'easy does it' grinding.

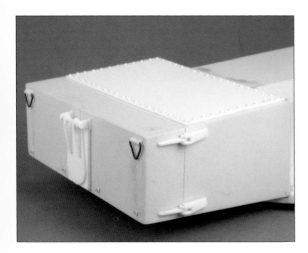

The large hinges added on the right side of the hull and the spent-casing ejection door are added. The punch and die set got a workout on the turret roof.

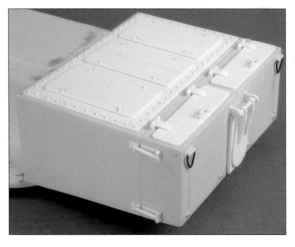

Locking clasps are added to the left edge of the swing away rear panel.

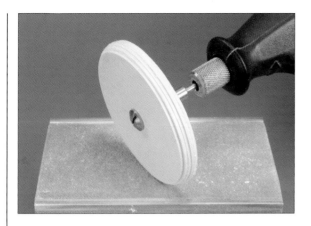

ABOVE, ABOVE RIGHT AND BELOW LEFT The sequence to build the bevelled smoke grenade banks turned out to be the most difficult part of the turret. First, a disc of laminated styrene the appropriate thickness was chucked into a Dremel and the upper and lower bevels were roughly shaped. Next, a No. 11

blade was used to get a smooth level surface. Lastly, only the extreme outer edge of the disc was cut away and holes for the SGLs were drilled. This was the only way I could figure out how to get mirror-image matching units.

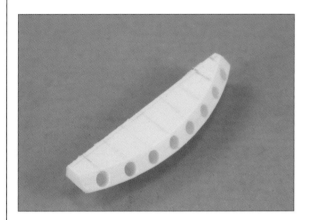

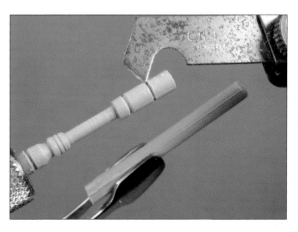

The primary sight, hatches and episcopes were built from scratch.

Weld beads made from thin stretched sprue, tacked on with liquid cement, and then textured with a soldering iron on very low heat.

A wind sensor was turned using my Dremel, using a short length of spare sprue and a Tamiya scriber.

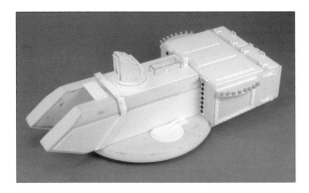 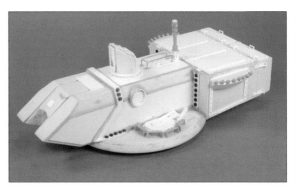

ABOVE AND ABOVE RIGHT The turret with a few more details added. The grenades are spares from an M113 kit while the large black bolts are from a CMK set. The wind sensor guard is brass wire and the episcopes are from the spares bin.

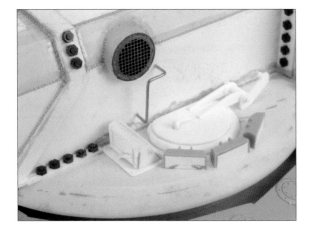 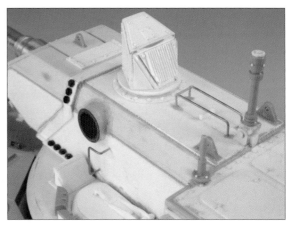

ABOVE AND ABOVE RIGHT Bent brass wire forms the turret grab handle to help the troops down into the hatch. The fins on the sight are for cooling, and are a complete guess on my behalf!

my parts to an exact fit. Instead, it is much easier to cut one part the right size, and cut everything else too large and just sand and hack it back to fit – that's what sandpaper and putty are for.

With the rough shape of the turret worked out, I built the gun mount using some Apoxie Sculpt and the base of a Rheinmetall 120mm gun from a Leopard tank. The Falcon uses a Ruag 120mm gun and, while it is not exactly the same as the one I've used, it is pretty close. The gun is from Modelpoint USA and is done very nicely; I've yet to be disappointed by anything from Modelpoint.

The base of the turret was made from stepped discs of .040in. plastic card laminated with a generous amount of CA. After clamping for a few minutes, I used a long cylinder cutting bit to grind a bevel into the outer edge. The trick here was to go very, very slowly.

I began to detail the turret rear with some thinner (white) plastic card, adding some lifting eyes from wire bent into a triangle, and the spent-casing ejection port, which throws the brass a fair distance. Some hinges and hinge latches were added to the rear side, as this large part swings away to allow for maintenance and restocking of the twin autoloaders. I scribed a line around this door rather than build the actual extension. On the turret roof I added a set of access panels for the autoloader while the punch and die set earned its keep creating bolt heads.

I made a wind sensor from a section of sprue chucked into my Dremel tool and turned at a low speed against a Tamiya scriber; this gets mounted on the

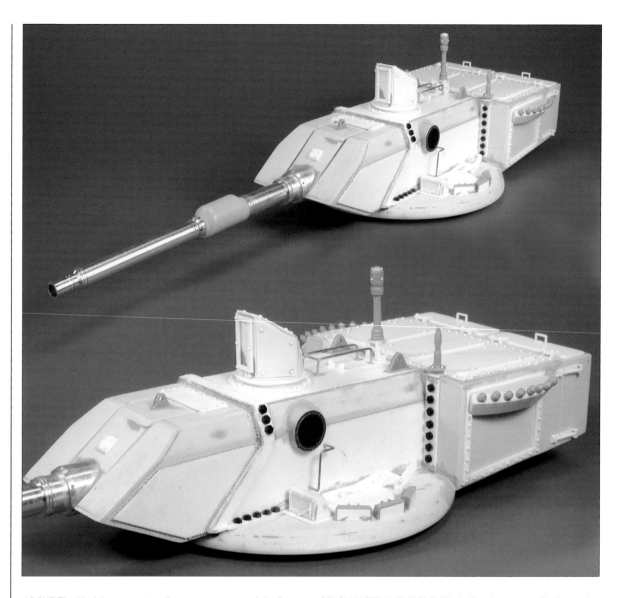

ABOVE The Modelpoint gun is a close approximation of the Ruag 120mm version. It might be a bit too long, but I did not want to chop an aluminium barrel for the sake of a few millimetres!

BELOW LEFT AND RIGHT The hull is the generic Challenger 1 (Al Hussein) with side skirts replaced with sheet styrene and brass tie-downs.

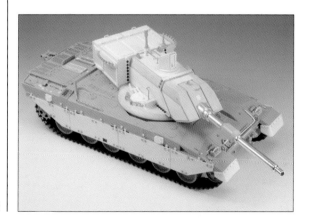

Smoke grenades from an M113 kit and Antenna mounts from a Merkava finish off the turret.
Some aluminium mesh from Scale Scenics was added to the engine deck.

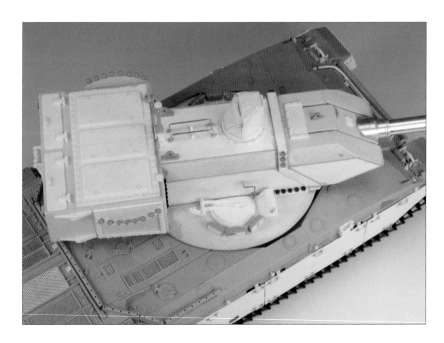

turret roof. At the rear of the turret roof are dual banks of Smoke Grenade Launchers (SGLs) mounted in a circular bracket with a compound bevels. I tried many ways to make two identical mounts, and nothing was working. Eventually, I made a large circle with an outside diameter that matched the radius of the SGL bracket. From there, I laminated some five sheets together, drilled a hole in the centre and mounted it in a Dremel. I spun the discs against a sanding block to get the top and bottom bevel and cleaned the edge up with the back side of an X-Acto blade. With the correct radius, I then sliced off two small chunks from each edge. With the correct shape, all that was left to do was drill eight evenly spaced holes to insert the smoke grenades into. This brings me to another point about scratch building – the tough part is not really making the part – it's figuring out how to make the part!

I made the gunner's sight based on a few pictures, but I had none of the back side. Some cooling fins added to the rear seemed a reasonable stretch of artistic licence. The hatches were made from laminated plastic card with a rounded edge bevelled using a file. The front windows are larger than the side ones, and were scratch built with a small wiper blade added. Side plates on the turret were cut from .015in. plastic card and edged with thin stretched sprue textured with a soldering iron. The roof also had a similar panel added; however, I tried making the weld beads using putty textured with a curved tube. I couldn't get it to look fine enough, so I ended up replacing it with the stretched-sprue welds.

On the left side of the turret there is a large circular vent that was made with tube and capped off with some etched mesh. Under this is a bent grab handle for the crewmen to raise and lower themselves out of the hatches. The rest of the crew episcopes came from the spares box. A few bolt heads, weld beads and antenna mounts, and the turret was complete. I won't go into the building of the hull as it follows pretty much the same process as the Cr 1 Mk 3 earlier in the book.

Painting and weathering

The only Falcon 2 I have seen is painted in desert tan and nearly devoid of markings. However, the Cr 1s in active service with the Jordanian Army are camouflaged in a unique three-tone scheme of green, khaki and red-brown. I decided to paint this prototype as if it were in regular service, adapting the paint scheme and markings worn by the Cr 1s.

First I primed the metal gun barrel with a shot of auto lacquer, as I find acrylic paint sometimes has a difficult time sticking to a polished surface. The primer gives a bit of tooth for the paint and won't react with the metal or resin parts of the barrel. I also primed the tank in flat black to give the colour coats the same tone. I didn't want to chance having the yellow plastic somehow change the colour of the camouflage paint. While I had the black out, I added a few drops of brown to the mix, and sprayed the tracks. Once done, I masked off the roadwheel contact strips.

I adapted the Al Hussein camouflage pattern to the Falcon. The base khaki colour is a mix of Gunze Hemp and IAF Green, which was sprayed over the whole kit and roadwheels. Next I sprayed the wood brown and then the green. I used a Badger 200 single action for this job, and you can see from the pictures that at this point there is a fair amount of overspray. To cut back on that, I mixed up small amounts of the base colour and then brown, and touched up the edges using a Tamiya SF airbrush.

Thinned dark-brown streaks were applied, as were lightened mixes of each camouflage colour. The original camouflage colours were heavily thinned and then reapplied over this layer in successive coats to lessen the effect of the shading. At this point I did all the brush painting of the black bits, fire extinguishers and the stencils for the unit markings. I think there should be an Arabic number on the black square on the glacis, but I was unable to determine exactly what it was from the reference photos. So, I just left it black. Once the detail painting was done, a wash composed of thinner and raw umber oil paint was applied with a 0 brush. I left the model under some lamps overnight, and then flat coated it with acrylic Polly-S the next day.

A bit of wear and tear in the form of paint chips along the edges and around the driver's hatch, plus some exhaust stains, fuel spills, streaks and some drybrushing on the tools and the model was nearly done.

I 'painted' the tracks with several shades of Mig Pigments and brown pastels. These were given the same oil wash and a very light drybrushing with chrome silver around the guide teeth. Ground-up pastel chalks sealed with Tamiya thinner were used for the roadwheel mud, while some dry pastels were brushed into the recesses and around the exhaust ports. Some MV lenses and foil optics were glued in place and the whole model was again given a Polly-S flat coat, only this time with a drop of Tamiya Buff added to tone down some of the weathering effects. Black Mig Pigments were wiped onto the track pads using a Mk 1 fingertip and the model was complete.

Vinyl tracks are first given a coat of black/brown, and then masked off along the roadwheel contact patch. After this, a reddish-brown mix is sprayed on, followed by a dark brown wash, a light brown drybrush and, in some spots, a steel dry brush.

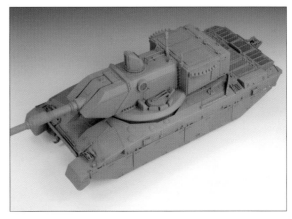

Painting begins with a coat of black primer.

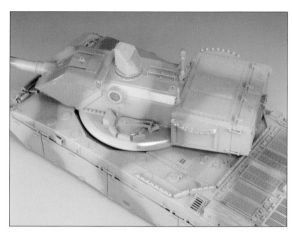

Then a mix of Gunze H336 Hemp and H312 FS34227. The Al Husseins are painted in a three-tone scheme unlike any other army I have seen.

ABOVE AND BELOW LEFT Broad bands of H37 Wood Brown are applied followed by accents of H340 34097. The overspray here is due to the wide setting on the airbrush which helps get the paint on fast.

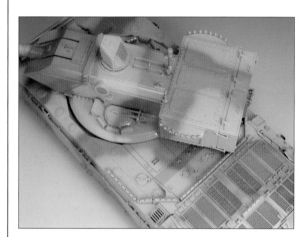

The camouflage pattern gets a tightened demarcation using the base colour and the brown shot through a Tamiya SF at roughly 10psi.

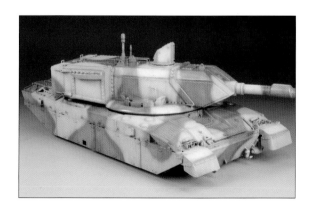

Dirty brown streaks and lighter faded spots get added using the Tamiya SF.

This effect gets toned down using diluted base colours.

After detail paint of fire extinguishers, unit markings etc., a dark-brown oil wash was applied.

A coat of flat acrylic brought the colours back to their original lightness.

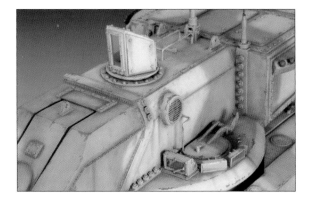

Coloured foil replaced the black painted optics.

Paint chips were added using a 2B pencil, and pigments were applied dry to give a streaked effect. The markings were painted with the airbrush using stencils cut from Tamiya tape.

Looking like something out of Star Wars, the Falcon model proved to be a very enjoyable project, despite not having many references or any scale drawings to build from.

Gallery

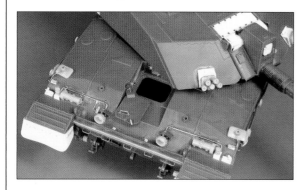

The Trumpeter kit can be brought up to a decent standard with the addition of a few scratch-built details and the Accurate Armour upgrade.

Fender formed from thin sheet and copper wire tie-downs plus wiring for the lights help improve the Trumpeter kit.

ABOVE AND ABOVE RIGHT **AA** fuel drums, roadwheels and hatches add extra detail.

BELOW Blast Models make an excellent Challenger crew. Signs are from Mig Productions and show a Cr 2 on exercise somewhere in Germany or Poland.

A mix of deck tan and buff paint is hazed along the lower hull to give a dusty look. The
Trumpeter kit is a challenge to build, but with the AA set can be made into a decent model.

Further reading

Böhm, Walter, *Challenger 1 & 2*, Concord Publications 7505, 2000

Debay, Yves, *Blitzkrieg in the Gulf*, Concord Publications 4001, 1991

Dunstan, Simon, *Challenger Squadron*, Crowood Press, 1999

Dunstan, Simon, *New Vanguard 23: Challenger MBT 1982–1997*, Osprey, 1998

Dunstan, Simon, *New Vanguard 112 Challenger 2 MBT 1987–2006*, Osprey, 2006

Foss, Christopher, *Jane's Armour and Artillery*, International Thomson Publishing, 1995

Katz, Samuel, N., *British Forces in Babylon*, Concord Special Ops 5225, 2003

Morrison, Bob, *Op Desert Sabre: The Desert Rat's Liberation of Kuwait*, Concord Publications, 1991

Morrison, Bob, *Desert Sabre: The Desert Rat's Liberation of Kuwait*, Concord Publications, 1991

Nicholls, Marcus, 'British Bulldog', *Tamiya Model Magazine International*, 106, 2004

Pollard, Spencer, 'Here's a Challenger Too & And Then There Was 2', *Military In Scale*, 143, October 2004

Schulze, Carl, *Britain's Challenger 2 MBT*, Concord Assault 7805, 2003

Tapsell, John, 'Updating the Challenger', *FineScale Modeler*, September 2000

UN Peacekeeper Recognition Guide Volume 1, Field Logistics Support Ltd, 1998

Armour modelling websites

www.missing-lynx.com
www.armorama.com

Reference websites

Walk around pictures of Challenger tanks: www.primeportal.net
Photos of British Operations: www.operations.mod.uk
Photos of Falcon 2 Turret: www.kaddb.com
Jane's Military Vehicles & Logistics: jmvl.janes.com

Kits and accessories

Injection-moulded Challenger kits

Manufacturer	Product number	Details
1/35 scale		
Accurate Armour	K053	Challenger 2
Accurate Armour	K053AG	Challenger 2 Op Telic
Modelcraft	359004	Challenger 1
Tamiya	35154	Challenger 1
Tamiya	35154	Challenger 1 Mk III
Tamiya	35274	Challenger 2
Trumpeter	323	Challenger 2 Op Telic
Trumpeter	345	Challenger 2 KFOR with Dozer
Trumpeter	308	Challenger 2 (also reboxed as Hobbycraft 6003)
1/72 scale		
Dragon Models Ltd	7228	Challenger 2 Iraq 2003
Dragon Models Ltd	7222	Challenger 2 KFOR
Revell	3120	Challenger 1 KFOR
Revell	3110	Challenger 1
Revell	3163	Challenger 1 with British Infantry
1/76 scale		
Matchbox	PK178	Challenger 1

Detail sets

Manufacturer	Product number	Details
1/35 scale		
Accurate Armour	C019	Challenger 1 Extra Armour
Accurate Armour	C020	Challenger Fuel Drums
Accurate Armour	017	5-gal Oil Drums
Accurate Armour	016	7.62mm GPMG Ammo Boxes
Accurate Armour	C081G	Challenger 2 Up-Armour set Op Telic
Accurate Armour	C081K	Challenger 2 Up-Armour set KFOR
Accurate Armour	C082	Challenger 2 Thermal Exhaust Covers
Accurate Armour	C086	Challenger 2 Enhanced Armour Iraq 2005
Accurate Armour	A032	Challenger Combat Dozer
Accurate Armour	C024	Challenger ARRV Conversion (for Tamiya)
Accurate Armour	A028	120mm UK Tank Ammunition
Accurate Armour	A029	120mm UK Tank Ammunition Boxes
Accurate Armour	A053	Challenger 2 Update Set (for Trumpeter)
Accurate Armour	A053G	Challenger 2 Op Telic Update Set (for Trumpeter)
Accurate Armour	A053K	Challenger 2 KFOR Update Set (for Trumpeter)
Accurate Armour	A053T	Challenger 2 Turret Upgrade Set (for Trumpeter)
Accurate Armour	A040	British Modern Tow Cables
Accurate Armour	A018	British Modern AFV Bin Set
Accurate Armour	A075	Challenger 2 Combat ID Panel Set
Accurate Armour	A084	Challenger 2 Perforated Wheels
Accurate Armour	A085	Challenger 2 Damaged Wheels
Accurate Armour	A073	Challenger 2 Plain Dished Wheels
Accurate Armour	A086	Challenger 2 Spare Wheels
Accurate Armour	DE17	Challenger 1 Decals
Accurate Armour	DE024	Challenger ARRV Decals
Accurate Armour	DEK053	Challenger 2 Decals
Accurate Armour	DEK053G	Challenger 2 Op Telic Decals
Archer Dry Transfers	35177	UNPROFOR Markings
Armour Track Models	00308	Challenger 2 Track (for Trumpeter)
Bison Decals	35007	Challenger 2 Iraq 2003
Bison Decals	35008	Challenger 2 Op Telic 2003-2004
Blast Models Resin	35055	Modern British Tank Crew
Echelon Fine Details	T35002	Challenger 1 Mk III IFOR/KFOR decals
Eduard Photo-Etch	35332	Challenger 1 Mk III (for Tamiya)
Eduard Photo-Etch	011	Challenger 1 Screens (for Tamiya)
Eduard Photo-Etch	35743	Challenger 2 Desert (for Tamiya)
Eduard Photo-Etch	076	Challenger 2 Desert (for Tamiya)
Eduard Photo-Etch	35565	Challenger 2 (for Trumpeter)
Eduard Photo-Etch	35733	Challenger 2 KFOR (for Trumpeter)
Eduard Photo-Etch	070	Challenger 2 KFOR (for Trumpeter)
Eduard Photo-Etch	35601	Challenger 2 Combat ID Panels
Extratech Photo-Etch	35023	Challenger 2 (for Tamiya)
Friulmodellismo metal workable tracks	81	Challenger 1 Tracks
LionMarc Model Designs	20000	Challenger 2 Barrel
Tamiya	35277	Challenger 2 Screens
1/72 Scale		
CMK Resin	065	Challenger 1 Equipment Set, Modern British Equipment,
CMK Resin	060	
CMK Resin	062	Tent Packs
Eduard Photo-Etch	22066	Challenger 2 Iraq
Eduard Photo-Etch	22073	Challenger 2 KFOR
Extratech Photo-Etch	72079	Challenger 2 (for DML)
Extratech Photo-Etch	72005	Challenger 1 (for Revell)

Index

Figures in **bold** refer to illustrations

AA kits 45–52
aerials 19, 20
air ID flags **18**, 19
air ID panels 12, **13**
ammo **18**
ammo cans and bins 12, **14**
Apoxie Sculpt, working with 19
armour
    appliqué **6**, 7
    side **26**, 38, 46
    stand-off 53, 55, **56**, **59**, **61**

bazooka plates 7
brush guards 35

cam nets and bins 12, 25, **25**
    painting 13
Carswell, Jim 53
chains, recovery 47, 49
Challenger (Cr) 1: origins and upgrades 5
Challenger (Cr) 1 Mk 3 3
    4th Armoured Brigade 24–31
    KRH 5–16
Challenger (Cr) 2
    Desert Challenger 2 32–44
    origins and upgrades 17
    Royal Dragoon Guards 53–63
    Royal Scots Dragoon Guards 17–23
Challenger (Cr) 2E 32
Challenger Armoured Repair & Recovery Vehicle (CrARRV) 45–52
chisels, filing down 54, 55
CIPs 18
cranes 49
cupolas 12

decals and markings
    Cr 1 Mk 3 9, 12–15, **13**
    DML 20, **20**
    Echelon 12–15, **13**
    painting **73**
    Revell 27
    UNPROFOR vehicles 46
decks
    detailing 8, 10
    painting 13
    replacing engine 32, **33**
    screens 8, 10, **10**, **54**
DML kits 17–23
dozer blades 5, 8, 10
    painting 13, 15, 46, **49–50**
Dremels, controlling speed of 6–7
drill holes, positioning 54, 55

episcopes 20, **66–67**, 70

Falcon 2 AB9C5 64–75
fenders **76**

figures **76–77**
fire extinguishers
    mounts 56
    painting 20, 46
fuel-can brackets and straps 10–12, 25–26
fuel drums 25, **26**, 35, **36**, **76**
    mounts 6–7, **6**, **33**, 34
    painting 27, **27**
    straps **13**, **18**, 19, **33**

glacis plates 7, 10
grab handles 8, 10, 19, **67**, 70
grenades **67**
    see also Smoke Grenade Launchers
grilles and covers 10, 19, **54**
guns 19, **34**, **36**, 38
    enhancing strap details 12, **14**
    Falcon 2 **65**, 67, **68**
    mounts 38, **62**, **65**, 67
    painting 15, 20, 27, **28**, **50**, **62**, 71

hatches **66**, 70, **76**
hydraulic hoses 47

lenses see lights: lenses; optics: glass simulation
lights
    guards 7
    headlight mounts 10
    indicator 7, 10
    lenses 19, **41**
    painting 20, 57
    wiring **18**, **56**, **76**

maps 14
mud flaps 7, 10, 38

Oehler, Robert 19
optics
    glass simulation 12, **14**, 20, **34**, 38, **40**
    painting 27, **28**, 46, **50**, 57, 58

painting and weathering
    camouflage patterns 12, **13**, 71, **72**
    dust and mud effect **14**, 20, **41**, 42, **50**, 57–60, **59–61**, 71
    exhaust stain effect 27, **41**, 42, **50**
    exposed metal effect **14**, 15
    fuel spill effect 15, **50**
    heavy weathering 46, **49–50**
    non-skid texture 53–55, **54**
    paint chip effect 15, 19, **20–21**, 27, **28**, 42, **73**
    'realistic' weathering 57–60, **58–61**
    rust effect 46, 49
parts: cutting to fit 64–67
Polly-S Flat 42

Revell kits 24–31
roadwheels

AA **76**
    desert's effect on **34**, 38
    making 46
    painting **41**, 42
    stored on CrARRVs **49**
rounded edges, making 10

sand skirts **18**, 19
sanding techniques 6–7
SGLs see Smoke Grenade Launchers
sights 5, **34**, 38, **66–67**, 70
signs **76**
Smoke Grenade Launchers (SGLs) 19, **66**, 70
sponsons **33**, 34
storage bins
    Cr 2 vs Cr 1 **29–30**
    CrARRVs 46, **47**
    Extratech 25
    front 25–26
    painting 27, **28**
    side 10, 12, 25–26
    turret 9, 10–12

Tamiya kits
    Cr 1 Mk 3 5–16, 45–52, 64–75
    Cr 2 (Desertized) 32–44, 53–63
tarps 10, 12, **18**, 19–20
TECs **18**
Thermal Imaging Sights (TIS) **34**, 38
Thermal Observation and Gunnery Sights (TOGs) 5
tie-downs **76**
    attaching **6**, 7
    tarps **18**, 19
    turret 8, 12
tight places, accessing **54**, 55
TIS see Thermal Imaging Sights
toolboxes **50**
tools
    maintenance **9**, 12
    painting 40
    pioneer 10, **33**
towing equipment 7, **7**, **33**, 35, **37**, 38
tracks 17, **36–37**, 38
    painting 24, 25, **41**, 42, 71, **71**
Trumpeter kits **76–77**
turn signals 35
turrets
    detailing **8–9**, 10–12
    Falcon 2 64–67, **65–67**

ventilation systems: Desert Cr 2 32, **33**, 34–35, **35**

water bottles 14
water-jug brackets 35
welded-on effect 11, 12
wheels see roadwheels
winch cables **48**
wind sensors **66–67**, 67–68

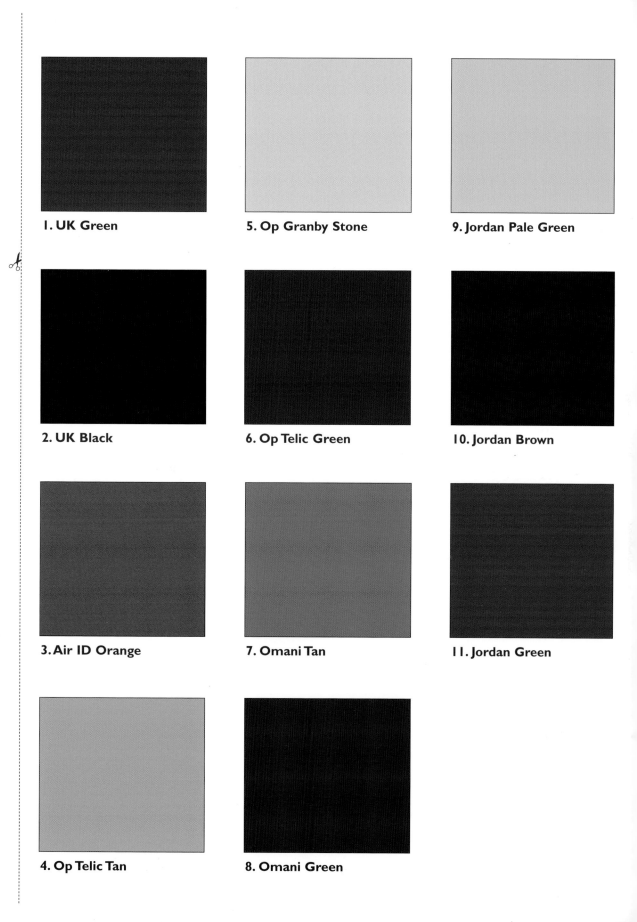

1. UK Green

5. Op Granby Stone

9. Jordan Pale Green

2. UK Black

6. Op Telic Green

10. Jordan Brown

3. Air ID Orange

7. Omani Tan

11. Jordan Green

4. Op Telic Tan

8. Omani Green

9. Jordan Pale Green

This base colour for the Jordanian scheme was made with a mix of Gunze H336 Hemp and H312 Pale Green (FS 34277). The aim was to mix a khaki colour that looked neither too brown, nor too green. It is similar a faded version of Testors' SAC Bomber Tan FS 34201.

5. Op Granby Stone

The Op Granby Stone colour was mixed using Tamiya XF-59 Desert Yellow, XF-57 Buff, and XF-19 Sky grey in a 4:1:1 ratio. Testors' British Armour Stone is also a good mix straight from the bottle.

1. UK Green

This colour is made with a mix of Tamiya XF-67 NATO Green and XF-62 Olive Drab. I'm told that tank crews are issued this colour in a concentrated paste form and use a number of different solvents to thin the paint for application. This practice results in a variety of greens.

10. Jordan Brown

This is simply Gunze H37 Wood Brown, similar to FS 30070.

6. Op Telic Green

In 2005, British forces repainted the tan Challenger 2 in an overall green. From the limited pictures I have seen of Iraq-based Cr 2s with the up-armour package, this green appears to be different from the UK-based Cr 2s. I used Tamiya XF-26 Deep Green, which, after weathering, seemed a good match. FS 34097 seems a good approximation.

2. UK Black

This is simply XF-69 NATO Black. If you don't have access to NATO Black then flat black mixed with dark grey will work.

11. Jordan Green

This is Gunze H340 FS 34097, Similar to Tamiya XF-58 Olive Green.

7. Omani Tan

With only four colour photos of Omani Challengers to go by, I reckoned that Tamiya XF-59 Desert Yellow was close match. This colour is similar to FS 30371.

3. Air ID Orange

Some of the Air ID panels I saw in Bosnia were painted with fluorescent orange paint, similar to FS 38903. However many just used a gloss orange that quickly lost its lustre. In this case, I used Tamiya XF-3 Flat Yellow with a few drops of XF-7 Flat Red.

8. Omani Green

Gunze H48 Field Grey 2.

4. Op Telic Tan

In many photos, the Op Telic tan seems to lean towards a yellow, much more so than the Op Granby tans. This shade was mixed with three parts Tamiya XF-60 Dark Yellow to one part XF-3 Flat Yellow. Most Op Telic vehicles exhibited a large amount of wear and chipping. Gunze G203 would also work.